DEAD DRAW [ded drô]: A <u>drawn</u> position in which neither player has any realistic chance to win. A dead draw may refer to a position in which it is impossible for either player to win (such as <u>insufficient material</u>), or it may refer to a simple, lifeless position which would require a major <u>blunder</u> before either side would have a chance to win.

Dead Draw definition retrieved on October 15, 2013 from the Wikipedia Glossary of Chess
<u>http://en.wikipedia.org/wiki/Glossary_of_chess</u>

To my husband, Rob, for his unfailing support during all the adventures I lead us into. To Michelle, Ryan, Meaghan, Cody and Ryder for being uniquely yourselves and being there for one another through all the challenges that a family encounters – may love always triumph! For Caleb, who continued to believe in us. For Mandi who always gets me to leave my comfort zone…Love forever and always…Kathy

To my family and friends, who helped me through my darkest times. To my mom, who was by my side constantly. And to Caleb, the light at the end of the tunnel. xoxo Mandi

It's always hard to be the first to discover darkness where we wish there could only be light; and it is a difficult journey to be the ones who can't stay silent about that darkness. We are not researchers or investigative journalists—we are a couple of women, a mother, Kathy, and grown daughter, Mandi, from Canada. The story you are about to read reveals what we found, inadvertently, when we encountered the real world of the 'Orphanage Business' in Ghana. Almost 5,000 innocent and vulnerable children are currently housed in unlicensed, private owner-operated Ghanaian orphanages. We returned from Ghana adamant about one thing; now was the time to shine a spotlight on what we had discovered.

We planned to go to Ghana to participate in the process of securing a legal, private adoption. At the time, the Canadian government was investigating allegations of child trafficking and bribery within adoption processes between Canada and Ghana. Most importantly, our family wanted a legal adoption with no compromises. We expected to accomplish this with help from the operators of the orphanage in question, who had already enthusiastically offered us their full cooperation. Mandi had volunteered with them on an earlier trip to Ghana and they were both overflowing with goodwill to assist us through the entire process. Later, when these operators finally realized no amount of a 'standard bribe' would be paid, we became immersed in the dark side of doing business with these Child-Dealers; a term we feel is much more accurate to describe them.

Who are Child-Dealers? They are business people, like the ones we became involved with, who profit from operating private orphanages in Ghana. Under the guise of running ethical, charitable organizations, Child-Dealers line their pockets with donated dollars, sell donated supplies for profit, and compete for the fees volunteers pay to participate in a work experience with them. Our term for these unethical acts is 'donation-hijacking'; it is rampantly practiced and is highly lucrative. In short, it pays big bucks.

Recent government statistics show that about 90% of the children housed in unlicensed orphanages of all sizes in Ghana, are neither orphaned nor abandoned. Make no mistake, innocent children drive the profits of this unregulated business sector, as they become the human-billboards of false advertising to attract foreign funding and support. Our time in Ghana allowed us to uncover this shocking devaluation of children and the way in which they are treated as mere commodities and nothing more.

When Child-Dealers house a child who is to be adopted, they expect to receive a big payment for the 'sale' of one of their commodities, and some will go to frightening lengths to prevent children from being adopted legally, when people, like us, refuse to pay them these bribes.

Our experience was shocking, dangerous, and traumatizing to not only the two of us, but to the child involved. We unexpectedly endured experiences so ugly; they fall far outside the norm of most tourists' experience when they travel to Ghana. Some readers will be unwilling to accept parts of our story because it is so antithetical to the beautiful, friendly Ghana most tourists experience. We've lived with criticism or mere dismissal of our experiences in Ghana as unlikely exaggeration or preposterous fiction. We accept and understand the reticence of skeptics. After all, when some of us buy a chocolate bar here in the West, we don't want to think about the proven fact that child slavery is heavily used to harvest cocoa beans. Some of us also avoid wondering if the diamond on our grandmother's engagement ring is what's now commonly called a blood diamond.

Child-Dealers continue to attract donor dollars and supplies from foreign sources, for example people like you and me. When the word 'orphanage' is used, the majority of us can't help but make assumptions—most of which are false. We would like for this book to help put an end to those assumptions.

Even though writing this book about our experiences was at times a painful emotional process, it has never been an option for us, as Rondeau women, to remain silent. When a light beam slices through darkness, it can become a pathway and instigator for change and that was our intention; to write a book that will put a metaphoric flashlight into the hands of as many people as possible. Help us shine more light on those Ghanaian children whose fate lies in the hands of unscrupulous and uncaring orphanage owners who use these children for personal profit. No child in Ghana should have to live beyond the reaches of

Ghanaian and international lawmakers, as these children are forced to do.

We have written *Dead Draw* for all the vulnerable children who are subjected, on a daily basis, to all that exists within the darkness of the 'Orphanage Business' in Ghana.

-Mandi Rondeau and Kathy Rondeau

Disclosures:

This is a creative nonfiction book. With regard to the degree of ambiguity that sometimes exists in the genre of creative-nonfiction, we offer the following disclosures to our readers:

To the best of our knowledge, we have written a truthful account of our experiences with the operators of the private orphanage that housed the child we adopted in an uncompromised, fully legal way.

All people are both participants and witnesses to their personal experiences. Truth and accuracy about a personal account is always limited to the perspective and memory of the person recounting their experiences. We have made every effort, between the two of us, to portray our experiences as accurately as we can. Nonetheless, we acknowledge that we are held to the limits of our perspective and memory. Therefore, we lay no claims of omnipotent authority over our complex subject matter.

Our experiences included interactions with many people whose roles were instrumental and we cannot exclude them from this account. We created aliases for all these parties, including those children at the orphanage who became involved in our experience. To protect the children there even further, we intentionally omitted descriptions of them beyond their age. We have also fictionalized the name and location of the orphanage that housed them.

As a work of creative nonfiction, we have inserted some minor fictitious characters into our story to improve the readability of some nugatory scenes. None are instrumental to our story in any way. Some segues between major sections of our story contain fictionalized content; however, they remain aligned with the emotional truth of our experiences. We have taken some artistic liberty to stylize content without affecting our goal for accuracy.

We wanted to minimize the use of the word 'orphan' in the body of our work for the following reason. The misuse of the word 'orphan' is, in our opinion, an intentional deception used by many owner-operators of these private orphanages, for the sole purpose of pulling at people's heartstrings in the hopes it will open their wallets. Only an estimated 10% of children housed in these orphanages (also called Children's Homes) are actually orphans, as you will soon find out. Finally, it would be remiss of us to omit mentioning that some people in this business sector provide extraordinary, kind and wonderful care for the children they house. However, according to the Ghanaian Department of Social Welfare (DSW), they are rare exceptions.

First Trip

July - August 2008

I wasn't always a bully trying to get my own way. But really, how could I help it if I didn't like cartoons like my siblings so obviously did? My sister, Michelle, was the reigning monarch during my youth (and really, she is still very bossy to this day). But on Saturdays, as soon as my mom left the room, I would go over to the TV and change the channel to World Vision or any program that showed little children with bloated tummies, bony limbs and wee brown faces with black flies buzzing about. I would sit there mesmerized as the narrators recounted the struggles of 'mud-hut children' facing daily hunger and the inability to afford the cost of attending school. I never missed a word of the repetitive appeals for donations and knew that when I had a job I would sponsor one of those kids. Heck, if only my parents paid me a decent allowance I would have done it then. The troubles that are visited upon the youth, right? Of course, my mom deemed the content of these programs as inappropriate for one as young as me (and my tattle-tale siblings) and she would come back into the room and try and direct me to more age-typical TV content. But let me tell you, even from an early age – once I have my mind set on something it's pretty hard to distract me from my end goal. With my first job, I sponsored one of those desperate little boys from World Vision and started volunteering with the Big Sisters program to help local children.

So now it is no surprise that I'm off to the African continent. Destination: Ghana. I signed up with an organization called 3W Volunteers, and now here I am on a plane bound for West Africa! Off I fly from Canada to my connecting flight in Amsterdam. As if the fates are against me, my flight is delayed. So I start to wander around the hot and muggy Amsterdam airport. Everywhere I look I see displays of wooden shoes in all sizes; from tiny ones small enough to fit the feet of a mythical wood fairy, to gigantic ones you'd need to haul home on a flatbed truck. Also competing for space were hundreds of cheeses that were also in every shape and size. Isn't it funny what we notice? Or what we have a hard time noticing? Like the airport signage – maybe things have changed in the meantime, but when I was there all I could think was that I should tweet The Amazing Race producers & suggest they use this airport as a fantastic challenge for the show contestants. It could be used to whittle down the number of teams pretty effectively. There are no boarding announcements, endlessly long waits in customs and only one person to check everyone's passports as we boarded our flight. Somehow we ended up being late by only forty minutes when we finally landed in Accra, Ghana.

When I got off the plane, I was immediately mesmerized by the concentrated ink-black darkness of the night. It loomed just beyond the airport terminal lights, as if a thick black cover was blanketing everything as far as I could see. I hadn't even taken a step forward when I was engulfed by the smothering humidity and heat. I remember thinking it felt like someone had instantly glued a steaming hot wet casing onto my skin—everywhere. And this was winter in Ghana. Daytime temperatures reliably reach 36 degrees Celsius (97 degrees Fahrenheit) or higher (although it feels like 40C or 104F) and everyone becomes coated with the musty smelling wet air produced by the extremely high humidity.

The Accra Airport is like no other I've experienced, and I'm a girl that goes places, so I like to think I sort of know. It seems that the only people permitted inside the airport are those who possess a passport and a plane ticket. Everyone else must wait outside behind a rope.

3W Volunteers said to wait to be picked up and no one seems to be here yet, so I people-watch to pass the time. All Ghanaians have striking looks; I don't think you will find a more beautiful race of people anywhere else. Everyone is so beautiful—perfect dark brown, shiny skin, great bone structure, well-kept hair, beautiful dark eyes with thick lashes and full lips that surround teeth so white you'd go broke trying to sell teeth whitening products here.

Time kept ticking by and I was beginning to wonder what to do next, when I finally heard my name called in a heavy Ghanaian accent. A lanky guy in his thirties approached me and asked if I was Mandi. When I answered yes, he chuckled and said, "Good! I guessed right! You are very, very light skinned!"

Of course, he was referring to my translucent white skin that stands out even more because I dye my light coloured hair black. If you put me in any crowd I can usually be counted on to have the palest complexion of all. Like a porcelain doll, with little designer clothes and matching shoes.

We start talking and he says his name is Cheech. Seriously? To describe Cheech I would say he has very well defined cheekbones, highlighted by shiny, spotless skin, sporting a small goatee under his lower lip. He's very charming and speaks with a nice welcoming tone of voice, even while chiding me for not sending him the photo I was supposed to. (I just got soooo busy preparing for this trip, it totally slipped my mind!) From head to toe, Cheech wears top brand label clothing, including an expensive looking Burberry ball cap pulled over a designer doo rag. I wondered to myself how a person could afford that kind of wardrobe by working as a tour guide. Regardless, I was so relieved we successfully rendezvoused. Cheech explains that he is my in-country coordinator and that he has been with 3W Volunteers for a few years now. He's to be my guide for all the tours that come with the volunteer package I paid for so I will be seeing lots of him in the weeks to come.

Cheech proceeded to inform me that I was the first of four volunteers he had to collect and the rest are set to arrive tomorrow. I ask him if I can borrow his cell phone so I can text home and let my family know that I have arrived and that I'm finally living out one of my dreams. Afterwards, we take a taxi from the airport to his house. I didn't see much of Accra because we drove through a maze of streets in almost total darkness—there are very few street lights. He ushered me into a small house reeking of mothballs. This tiny abode has small everything: living room, kitchen, and a closet-sized bathroom. It's sparsely furnished but he has a huge collection of pirated DVD's piled in stacks beside a really large TV. There's only one bedroom furnished with a double bed and a set of bunk beds, all with no blankets, only sheets.

By this time, I am really feeling the six hour time zone difference and am too exhausted after flying over 11,000 kilometers (6,835 miles) to summon the energy to worry about the fact that I was the only other person here. Oh well, my trusty instincts aren't raising any red flags about this guy. Cheech has plans to sleep on the living room floor, and so he does.

I was so grateful to climb into bed, but it was also my first night sleeping in a sauna seasoned with mothballs. There's a ceiling fan rotating above my bed but I think its sole function is to make me imagine it's supplying me with a smidgeon of relief even when it's not lowering the room temperature at all. I finally fall asleep feeling like I am still wearing a hot, humid casing. My final thought as I fall off to sleep is that I hope I get used to this. Little did I know I was going to think I would die of hunger before the heat got to me.

It isn't long into my second day that Cheech starts losing some 'charm points' with me. He insisted we couldn't eat until after he picked up the other volunteers. I don't know if that's because of a custom I have to abide by or if it's just his preference. I have not eaten an actual meal since arriving yesterday so I'm munching my way through my stash of Clif™ bars to stave off an early death from starvation.

My day started off rather weird because Cheech must have left me alone in the house at some point during the night. I know this because when I came out of the bedroom this morning, I met a delightful, new volunteer named Deidre. She has big round brown eyes, gorgeous long shiny brown hair, and a great figure. She's energetic, self-assured, and has a great personality. She asked Cheech if he could take us to a money exchange place before doing anything else today. Deidre was in dire need of a purse, so Cheech hired a taxi that took us to a typical Ghanaian open-air market.

It was just like the images you can find online. It had a dirt floor and most of the brightly colored wares were displayed on rickety wooden tables. Flies were buzzing around all the food items. The only shade came from roofing made of tarps or sheets of reclaimed rusty tin that were erected over some market stalls. As white people, each time we paused anywhere for longer than two seconds, Deidre and I were bombarded with the loud, incessant clamoring of twenty to thirty vendors, who all urged us to buy something from them. The noise level and crowds made for one very intense shopping experience.

After perusing the market, we went again by taxi to a mall. This mall was definitely an anomaly I didn't expect in Ghana. It was heavenly as it was air conditioned and filled with designer stores, movie theatres and even a food court! Cheech explained that because tourism is an important industry and Accra is where some very wealthy citizens live, there are a few places in this massive city that cater to the needs of those with lots of money to spend.

Deidre found herself the much needed purse. Cheech then informed us we would be allowed to swim in the natural pools at Wli Falls when we toured it and asked us if we'd each packed a swimsuit. I told them both I didn't need one because I was definitely not going to be swimming. I'm paranoid of slimy fish and parasites in fresh water lakes, and sharks in the ocean. Deidre though, wanted to buy one and Ghanaians don't use swimsuits, so finding a place in the mall that sold them was extremely difficult. After a long search we eventually discovered a Puma™ store that took credit cards and Deidre happily purchased a couple of tank tops and a bathing suit.

By now both Deidre and I were living off the Clif™ bars I'd brought with me and it was a consummate performance of good manners that prevented us from begging Cheech to stop and let us eat at the food court. Like many people, when I get hungry I can be a tad bit cranky, so it was with supreme effort that I continued to be polite to Cheech.

By now we are starving for an actual meal, we are in a taxi and it is dark out – so the whole day has gone by without us eating anything but our protein bars. We arrive at the airport to pick up the remaining volunteers only to find out that the flight would be delayed by two hours. Finally, finally, finally we get to eat at a small outdoor Chinese food restaurant. Cheech got a little weird when it came to the menu. He won't eat anything that's been in contact with onions or garlic—he claims it will taint his soul or something like that. I chose a chicken and rice dish, thinking, even dreaming that I would be eating within a few minutes. HA! Not so!

It took close to two hours for the food to arrive at our table, but the portions were huge, about three times the average size of portions we'd get in Canadian restaurants. I was ravenous so I made a good dent in my plate.

The other volunteers eventually arrived and you have to picture this—after they collected their luggage, the five of us have to squish into a tiny, two-door little taxi. (Everyone takes taxis here, like in New York). This thing had bucket seats in the front, but little room for two adults in the backseat—let alone four! Imagine being at a circus and watching an endless bunch of clowns exiting from a ridiculously small car. That's hilarious (well maybe not hilarious but it is kind of funny). There is nothing funny about this experience. The car's interior was dirty, sweaty, hot and to no one's surprise, minus seat belts too. We were wedged in like sardines and then had to pile all the luggage onto our laps. The trunk was almost nonexistent and so small it was useless to attempt to stow anyone's luggage in it.

The driver and Cheech sat comfortably up front and chatted away in Twi, the local language, while everyone in the backseat lost all feeling in our lower extremities thanks to the heavy luggage. The driver drove insanely, but we will get back to the driving conditions of Ghana in a bit.

It is pitch black when we arrive back at the mothball house. Now, all five of us will be sharing the teensy-weensy bathroom. Did I mention that there is only cold water to shower with? More importantly, cold water that the cockroaches don't seem to mind? Because I do forget to tell my mom some of these things before she makes the trip overseas. Which I'm almost certain she feels were very important factors to consider before committing. This eventually leads into a late night discussion in which, if I remember correctly, she threatens to murder me for omitting. Anyway, the shower stall has a really big window but conveniently lacks curtains, so anyone on the street can look in for their own show— it feels like showering on a sidewalk. Ugh!

Day three of the journey begins with Deidre leaving for The Last Hope Children's Home. It's her volunteer base for the next six weeks, and already I wish we had selected the same place to volunteer. It gets very dull right after she leaves and I spend most of my day in a trotro (what's a trotro you ask? Hold on a sec and I'll get to that). Technically, my day was focused on heading out on one of 3W Volunteer's guided tours. The destination was down south to the Cape Coast region to observe a native fishing ceremony. Cheech, dressed as usual in yet more top brand clothes, handed us (the remaining volunteers came too) over to a new guide. The ceremony was done in this region's native Twi language (Useful info: Twi and Fante are the two most common tribal languages spoken in the Cape Coast region of Ghana) and our guide deserted us without arranging for a translator. I'm beginning to suspect we are not dealing with professional grade tour guides… If asked, I'd give the whole day a big one star out of five. It was hot, humid and boring except when we walked along the beach with a swarm of excited children following us everywhere and calling out, "Obroni! Obroni!" (Pronounced Oh-bro-nee) which I later learn means white man in Twi.

Now, back to the trotros--figuratively and narratively. Trotros are stripped down, bare bone, fourteen passenger, narrow, mid-sized vans. There's no way they are officially fourteen seat passenger vans—more like factory made eight passenger ones. They have three bench seats in the back, each with a jimmied foldout seat that you pull up as you squish your way by to gain access to the next bench seat behind that one. Once a bench seat is full, the foldout seat is pulled back down to create an extra place for someone to sit. They expect four people to stuff themselves into these bench seats (these vans are really narrow), and look out if you end up as the unlucky passenger who has to sit on one of these foldout seats. They aren't stable in the least, and Martin, one of the volunteers, was bounced around like an overly energetic baby in a Jolly Jumper ® for the whole trip there, poor guy!

It's pretty clear that Ghana doesn't have vehicle inspections, because the trotros have boards on the floor as makeshift covers over rusted out holes the size of pies. After our tour, I strategically headed back to the trotro first so I could avoid one of the Jolly Jumper ® seats for the return trip!

Another aspect that only helped to make the hot, humid day even longer is that the trotros don't leave the station until they sell a ticket for every seat. Full capacity means two drivers, and at least a couple of goats and numerous squawking chickens tied onto the van's roof. Then, a dozen adults take their seats, some accompanied by kids of varying ages who will ride in the lap of whomever they are with. Apparently, people here consider it ludicrous to buy a child a seat of their own.

Any luggage you bring along has to stay on your lap or, for a price, they'll stow it away in the back or up on the roof. That is if there's enough metal left to hold it along with the menagerie that is already up there. Personally, I wouldn't opt for that because the odds are very high that whomever's luggage ends up on the roof, comes back down with lots of evidence that when goats and chickens are on a road trip and have to go, they just go. Yuck!

I still remember talking with a Ghanaian who had traveled to the USA—he said one of the strangest things he encountered in America was how busses and trains left at the posted times even if they were still almost empty! Gyuszi, a short charming volunteer from Hungary, with a great smile, told us this is his third stay in Ghana and that it's normal to wait a few hours for your trotro to fill before they pull out from the station. We were wondering if Cheech did some pre-arranging for us or maybe we were just getting lucky. At the beginning of our day, we only had to wait ninety minutes for the trotro to fill up. After a long, hot day though, we had to wait two hours for our trotro to fill to capacity for our return trip. When it finally left, it took us over three hours to travel the 145 kilometers (90 miles) back to Accra because the roads were so busy—mostly other trotros and taxis. Waiting is part of the Ghanaian culture so I've been learning to adapt as best I can.

If I were to look for something positive in this day, I'd have to say I'm thankful we were guided right up to the trotro when we were in that station because there are dozens of them waiting at the trotro stations, which seem to be as busy as Penn Station at rush hour. The stations are jammed with people and street vendors weaving through the crowds trying to sell their goods. Thank goodness for those vendors! We all bought some plastic bags of water, which are called water sachets here. Water sachets are small, five inch square plastic bags and you just bite off a corner to suck out the water, which is surprisingly fresh and delicious, unless you get the odd one that tastes like plastic. To our delight, we were also able to buy ice-cold cans of soda, which most of us used as mini cold packs on our bodies before quenching our thirst....I think we must have sweat out more than we drank because no one needed to stop for a bathroom break on the road home.

Did I mention the roads are beyond terrible here? They are filled with potholes and they look as if they've been target practice for aerial bombings during a recent war. That, along with the tons of garbage and the rusty carcasses of a scary amount of abandoned vehicles lining the roadsides, makes for little maneuvering space when our driver swerves to avoid goats no less than four times. His ninja driving skills pay off when he swerves to miss a car driving on the wrong side of the road. (In case my mom reads this, it only happened once and I obviously lived to tell the tale). Our ninja driver also used his slick swerving moves to avoid the pink chickens playing chicken on the road with us. (I'm so clever!) Now, about the pink chickens. Another volunteer, one of Gyuszi's pals, told us he'd heard that the theory behind the pink paint strategy is that hawks don't recognize pink colored chickens as a potential meal, therefore, they don't hunt them. Really? I can't help wondering if the pink paint being used is toxic to them and humans...Note to self – do not consume chicken while in Ghana. Of course, that was a short lived promise.

Somehow, hours later, we find ourselves safely back at the mothball house. The heat and humidity have completely zapped my energy. I form a plan: I'll shower and tumble into bed so I can fall asleep while still cooled off from the freezing cold water.

I forgot to mention that the other two volunteers who had been here with us went off to their volunteer destinations so everyone is gone now and I now have the bedroom to myself again. As I drift off to sleep I'm trying to decide if Cheech is a nice person or a swindler, out to nickel and dime us volunteers into the poor house. My instincts are telling me there's something shifty about him when it comes to money…just my personal opinion…hard to tell when I don't speak the language. We pay for the taxis, our food and his, and he has provided us with cell phones as he says it is cheaper to rent his phones than to purchase new ones. Oh well, tomorrow I'm off to Volta Farms to start my adventure so my bank account and I will both be safe. (Just kidding, mom, I'm going for dramatic effect here!)

It is day five and who would have guessed that in Ghana I would have so much time to just read and read and read and read? I arrived here at Volta Farms yesterday. My trotro trip was supposed to take about two hours to travel the 145 kilometer (90 miles) distance. Of course, the trip did not start until after a two hour wait at the trotro station for it to fill to capacity with passengers and a roof full of chickens and kids. (The baby goat type of kids were on the roof, not the human ones.)

The roads were just as bad going north as they had been in the south. Now I know why most of the trotros have no bumpers; they don't survive some of the deep potholes. We were almost halfway to Volta Farms when the police at the Kpong checkpoint refused to let us pass. Apparently, the trotro's sole license plate had gone missing during our jolting ride so we had to backtrack at half speed for a good hour before it was spotted and fastened back on. Back to the last checkpoint we went. There are a lot of police check points on all the roads throughout Ghana. It seems most of the time they just look around in the vehicle and then wave us through. There are some check points where anyone with passports are required to get out of the vehicle and have their passports checked over by the police.

In total, the necessary retrieval of the license plate tacked another 90 minutes onto our trip. I think the chickens were getting as cranky as we passengers were. Come to think of it, it might very well have been cooler traveling on the roof than inside the trotro. I was squished in very tightly with eleven other people and some children, and we were all sweltering in the heat and drippy humidity. I can't tell if the younger kids pee on their parent's lap or if sweat just accumulates underneath them. Everyone traveling with a child arrived at our destination with big wet blotches on their clothes where little bums had sat for the last three and a half hours in the trotro.

Ho is northeast of Accra, just 20 kilometers (12 miles) from the eastern border of Togo. This is a very picturesque region of Ghana. The scenery is nothing short of breathtaking. The flat plains of the coast had mostly mangrove swamps and short vegetation. The road we are traveling is taking us through a much denser, lush jungle rainforest. The terrain keeps getting steeper and steeper and it's decorated with many glistening small waterfalls.

Lake Volta is directly west of Ho, only about 25 kilometers (16 miles) as the crow flies. It is the largest man-made lake in the world, with an approximate surface area of 8,502 square kilometers (3,283 square miles) and accounts for almost one tenth of Ghana's entire surface area. It was created as an upstream reservoir when the construction of the Akosombo Hydroelectric Dam was completed in 1965. Farmlands in the dry Accra Plains, south of the dam, get irrigation from the lake that also sustains a major fishing industry. Although from afar, Lake Volta looks dazzling and inviting, it is quite polluted and therefore unsafe to swim in. Isn't it interesting how many things look good at first and then the more you know or see the less it can become? Deep words of wisdom here folks, but you aren't really paying for a self-help book so let's get back to my story.

Ho is the capital city of the Volta region. In my tourist guide, it says it has two hospitals, the newest built in 2000, lots of medical clinics, churches, a big Catholic Cathedral, and large sports stadiums. It is made up of eight suburbs that used to be eight different independent villages before they all amalgamated. To me, Ho looks more like one huge village that slowly bulged into the size a city. Only the interior streets are paved. All the connecting roads are typical red dirt roads and by now, I've accepted that the words: rough, bumpy, potholes, ruts, dusty and obstacle-strewn describe all the roads I need to travel on.

The city roads are lined with gutters almost 3 feet deep and 3 feet wide. They provide fast drainage during the powerful rainstorms that occur through the winter months. These deep gutters aren't marked or fenced in any way though, so if you don't want to fall into one it is advisable to watch where you are walking or driving at all times. I've been cautioned to be very careful to avoid them if I walk along streets after the sun goes down. Street lights are a rarity here and the nights are pitch black.

I was so excited to arrive at Volta Farms even if the trip took forever. Here at last is where I'm going to make a difference. With my culinary arts background and information from numerous nutrition courses crammed into my head, I'm pumped and eager to teach the farm workers and their families all about proper nutrition and hopefully work with children in the local school too. I've brought flash cards and soccer balls to win the children over—I have a plan and I can't wait to get started.

I was supposed to meet the program director, a woman named Vicki, but instead a male in his mid-twenties named Alex greeted me. He's very good looking and would have stood out in any crowd of male Ghanaians as tall, handsome, and muscular. Even though he struggled with English, he was friendly and very helpful as he showed me to the dorm and deposited my luggage in my room. The dorm is surrounded by a wire fence, presumably to keep livestock out. It's a large U-shaped building that contains eight bedrooms. Some are single rooms and some are large enough to hold up to four beds. Each of the bedrooms has its own bathroom, including the single bedroom that's assigned to me.

My room is adequately furnished. It has a bed, a desk, and a chair. The bathroom of course features a cold-water shower. This farm is funded by various churches in the southern USA and outside my bedroom window, through the trees, I have a view of the Volta Farms Church Chapel where local services are held on Sundays.

When supper is ready, Alex lets me know, so as soon as my luggage is stowed in my room I follow him to the kitchen building. He ushers me into a small room in an adjoining building that has a small wooden table and a rickety old chair. Apparently, as the sole white person here, I am to eat in this room alone. I don't understand why I am being segregated, but I take it in stride as part of my adventure here.

The cook, whose name I can't remember right now, is a large, tired looking woman. The skin on her hands is very rough and red, and she has the demeanor of a pleasant, but worn out person who's worked very hard all her life. She hasn't spoken a word of English to me. Nobody appears to know how to speak English here except Alex, even though it is supposed to be the official national language of Ghana.

I was tired from the day of travel, so I headed back to my dorm right after supper, trying my best not to insult Cook by leaving too much food on my plate. She'd served me a massive amount of white rice and mushrooms cooked in a spicy tomato sauce and sure enough, she didn't look pleased that I couldn't polish off a meal meant for a football linebacker. After I crawled into bed early (for me) I lay there enjoying how blissfully quiet it was to be the sole occupant of the dorm. I think I'm getting a little used to being hot and having wet skin ALL the time! It's definitely an uncomfortable feeling but I knew before I came here that I'd have to adapt to the heat and humidity one way or another.

As I begin day six of my adventure, I head to the kitchen where I know from yesterday's experience, breakfast will be waiting. Yesterday, for the entire day, I was really looking forward to a good cup of coffee. Imagine if you will, a cup, functional and a decent size, which Cook hands to me, filled with what I'm going to say was coffee. As I am inhaling the sort of familiar fragrant aroma I peer into the cup and notice clumps of small powdered milk curdles floating not so gracefully in the brown muddy looking water. Not quite the cup of coffee I was visualizing...

Needless to say I didn't dare complain about it for fear Cook would double the size of my breakfast. Oh, I almost forgot to mention... I pass on putting sugar in my coffee because it had what seemed to be a farm of ants crawling through it. It didn't seem possible for me to get sugar sans ants into my coffee, and I can't imagine scooping out ant-floatees from the surface of my morning coffee. If that's the norm here, I think I'll take a pass on 'going native' to that extent!

Speaking of ants, here at Volta Farms I've found the world's biggest anthills. Seriously! There are pillar shaped anthills as tall as six meters all over the place. And the ants are not just in the sugar. I've ditched wearing shoes because it's so frigging hot but the down side is that my feet are always covered in burning ant bites. Ants are everywhere—literally. Even while I shower, they attempt to crawl up my legs. At night, after I get into bed, I carefully tuck the very fine meshed mosquito netting in tightly under my mattress. Even that doesn't prevent rogue ants from visiting me during the night, and all are swiftly sent on to another reincarnation by none other than yours truly.

Anyway, my breakfast is a typical Ghanaian food called Kenkey (Pronounced can-ka). It consists of a mixture of compressed corn that had been boiled slightly before peanuts or other types of groundnuts were added to it. Then this mixture was wrapped in some kind of leaf, tied with string, and boiled until it became piping hot.

Joyce the Cook, (I remembered her name this morning), expertly unwrapped it and quickly rolled it onto my plate. It tasted like corn on the cob with peanut butter on it and was actually quite delectable. I thought breakfast was done, but Joyce appeared again with white bread, a boiled egg and two small bananas, all of which I ate, even though the Kenkey was very filling. Seems like I've gone from one extreme to another—first going for hours and hours without food on the first two days with Cheech, and now I feel like I'm being fed as if I'm a sumo wrestler in training. (Notice I'm pretty good with the metaphors?)

Vicki, the program coordinator was still a no show so I got tired of waiting around for her. I tracked down Alex and asked if I could tag along while he did his usual chores. First we passed by the baby goats and I was hoping we'd go in to feed them because they are the cutest animals ever, but Alex had already fed them earlier in the morning. Instead I learned to feed the rabbits. They are raised as a source of meat. There were about 150 of them with plenty of adorable babies. I would hate to raise rabbits. There's no way I could kill cute little bunnies so I'd probably go broke trying to feed the hundreds and hundreds and hundreds I'd eventually end up with. My mom has bunnies, a boy and a girl. She took them to the vet who gave them a stern talking to about the birds and the bees, did some minor surgery to make the visit worth the trip and they have remained just good friends with no benefits and therefore no risk of babies. It's all worked out for her.

Next, we fed the ducks, polar opposites of the cute bunnies. The whole flock of ducks smelled disgusting. I've never seen ducks so dirty. I wonder if they get that way because they have no place to swim. Don't ducks usually preen themselves immaculately? Anyway, that's certainly not the case with these ducks. Alex compared them to pigs and I have to say I concur. He also told me the farm is in the process of building the ducks a much bigger pen that will feature a large pond for them. That should give them a good makeover and hopefully take care of their disgusting odor too. (Note to self, no eating rabbit or duck either!)

I was excited about feeding the snails, so I asked Alex to take me to them. I had read up on them before coming here and thought it would be very cool to observe them. Ghanaian snails are the largest species in the world. They are the size of a computer mouse with a shell added and one is able to fill the palm of your hand! (Not that I'd ever volunteer to hold such a slimy creature.) Ugh!

Ghanaians are beginning to farm them as a food source. Once they are collected from the jungle they have to be contained in special, very fine wire-mesh pens. These snails will eat over 500 species of jungle plants, which makes them a serious threat to the native ecosystems. Alex took me to the pen but the limbs of a humungous, fallen tree were draped over it. The tree had missed the pen but all the snails were dead which seemed rather weird until Alex explained to me that they had starved to death because the workers believed the fallen tree was bad luck. No one fed the snails after the tree came down. I guess it will take a while for the workers here to learn how to farm snails for profit.

After that, we filled large baskets to the rim with fresh pulled long green grass and lugged them to the grass cutters pen. Grass cutters which are also known as cane rats, are the second largest rodent in continental Africa and considered quite a delicacy. In fact, Ghanaians are somewhat crazy about eating them. Alex tells me that if a vehicle driver sees one crossing the road, they purposely swerve to hit it and happily take the treasured carcass home for a feast. Yuck! But seriously, I saw them skinned and stretched out over BBQ pits in the market place and at the trotro stations. I guess it is quite an expensive food item so most Ghanaians just buy a small strip on a skewer for a quick and savory snack.

Grass cutters look like a beaver with some added rat DNA. They have coarse dark brown fur, long talons on their paws and huge long rat-like tails and beady rat eyes – maybe that's why they are also known as cane rats. Feeding them was our last chore of the day, so to pass the afternoon I Googled these creatures. I found out that farming them is actually saving the environment. Normally farmers wait until the native grasslands dry out and then set fires to kill the population of grass cutters that live and hide in the tall grass. They then take the charred carcasses home, skin them, and skewer them before placing them over large shallow outdoor BBQ pits. Unfortunately, these intentionally started fires become fast moving infernos that easily spread from the natural grasslands to farmers' crops in the area. In the end, crops and many other unlucky critters are wiped out. Farming cane rats is becoming very popular because of how it is saving crops, protecting the environment, and preserving several species of small animals.

It's a wonder no one has suggested that Ghanaians import giant anteaters from South America. This animal is a very popular food item there. Apparently, an adult anteater can slurp up over 30,000 ants a day and they live for over twenty years in captivity. I'm imagining a herd of slow moving anteaters, wearing collars and tinkle-bells like sheep, wandering from one ant pillar to another on Volta Farms, getting fat as they graze on ants day after day. It could be such a 'win-win' proposition.

The rest of my day was boring which is probably why my mind is coming up with ideas like importing anteaters. All I did was lounge on my bed reading one of the books I'd packed. Vicki didn't show up and I'm beginning to wonder if there's been some kind of communication break down between her and 3W Volunteers. Maybe she doesn't know I'm here. Oh well, I don't have anywhere else to go so I'll keep hanging out with Alex, feeding the Volta Farms menagerie while stuffing my face with the piles of food Joyce serves me.

So on Days Seven and Eight I'm still waiting for Vicki and therefore still bored. Doing chores with Alex doesn't take very long each morning. After that, I just wait. I can't fault Alex, as it isn't his job to entertain me. He's easy going and tries his best to converse with me in his broken English but he's busy all day with many responsibilities and I don't see much of him after joining him for his morning chores.

It seems I'm only popular with the ants. I still have not found anyone else here who speaks English, though I have tried to exchange hellos with everyone who works on the property. I'm still the only white person here and I'm frustrated that my plans are not coming to fruition. I'm feeling lonely and deserted here on a hot, muggy, dusty farm in a foreign country. It appears that my most important job while I am here is to keep Joyce, the hard working cook, smiling by eating platefuls of yams, fried plantain, and mountains of white rice topped with mushrooms drenched with a spicy tomato sauce.

On a more positive note, I'm adjusting a little better to the intense heat and humidity. This is no place for designer clothes and high heels, though. I wear loose clothing and respect their culture by dressing in clothes that cover me appropriately. (No shorts or short skirts). I wear a headband to keep the sweat from running into my eyes and like the locals, I take two showers a day to keep clean and to cool off. I don't know if I've mentioned this yet, but the dirt here (and throughout Ghana) is red and very fine. It is kicked up whenever I walk and then sticks to my damp skin. That's why it's hard to stay clean.

Oh, wonderful day eight! At last, Vicki arrives, pouring out apologies for her much delayed arrival. Ghanaians often have large families with whom they share many responsibilities and something was going on in that department for her. It is part of their culture. When she didn't offer a detailed explanation, I did not ask for one. It's hard to be mad at her because she's super nice and so friendly. She's a bit short like me and is a curvaceous, heavy-set attractive woman. In her forties, Vicki is always smiling as she chats to me in perfect English—which, needless to say, is music to my ears.

The first thing we did was take a ten minute walk up the dirt road to the public school. As soon as we approached the peach and brown painted building, some of the students came running up the road to meet us because it was their recess time. Here the region's tribal language is Ewe (Pronounced: "eh-way") and when these children started chanting, Yovo! Yovo! (Rhymes with "Go! Go!"), it brought even more school children out onto the road to greet us. One brave little boy, who only looked to be four years old, ran up and hugged my legs. Wow, was I in trouble after that, as all the other children tried to hug me at once. They were all so sweet!

We had come for an unannounced visit, but the teachers were all smiles as Vicki introduced me. We stayed for about an hour while I showed the children the flash cards I had brought for them. The flash cards provided a comical clash of cultures because they were Canadian made and had grizzly bears and beavers on them, which of course these kids had never seen. Then I gifted them the soccer balls I had brought, which they also thanked me for profusely. Vicki arranged for me to come back next week to spend more time helping out in the classrooms. In total, there were fifty children of varying ages in attendance and they all waved goodbye enthusiastically as we headed back to the farm.

The cutest thing happened when Vicki and I did the evening feeding of the bunnies. School must have ended for the day because half a dozen young school boys appeared and sat like statues on a bench to watch us. Vicki says all the children are fascinated by Yovos like me (white people), because they are raised to believe everything about living life as a white person is fantastic.

As I end my day tucked into my bed with mosquito netting safely cocooning the bed, I remember that in two more days I will be reunited with Deidre. We'll both be picked up, along with other volunteers, for more guided tours around the Volta region. I can hardly wait to hear how things are going at The Last Hope Children's Home, where she is volunteering.

Day nine has Vicki showing me how to harvest the oyster mushrooms, which are another source of income for the farm. Oyster mushrooms are grown in sealed bags of sawdust that have been inoculated with microscopic mushroom spores called spawn. The spawn are left to grow for months until the sawdust turns white from mycelia, the growth that produces a mushroom. These spawn bags are then bought by mushrooms farmers who stack them with the tied ends of the bag facing outwards, along the inside walls of a designated mushroom house. These spawn bags are tubular in shape. They are about 50 centimeters (20 inches) long and 20 centimeters (8 inches) in diameter when filled. Their uniform shape makes them stack very nicely on top of each other. Don't you love that I have all these random facts just thrown in here? It's like you are learning while being entertained… I am entertaining you am I not? Of course I am, or you would have stopped reading by now! Okay, back to being a writer. The mushroom house at Volta Farms was a small, closet-sized old wooden building. Its far wall was lined with a tidy stack of spawn bags, 20 bags wide, and 10 bags high. Some bigger operations have mushroom houses that contain a thousand or more spawn bags.

The wavy leaf shaped oyster mushrooms love the tropical climate that Ghana offers. They grow right out of the outward facing tied end of each bag. This made it very easy to pick the mushrooms that were ready to harvest, although we had to be very careful not to bruise any of the surrounding immature ones. We picked about a wheel barrow's worth and then washed them very gently before leaving them to dry while we went back and swept the dorm rooms that Vicki and I were using. Then we went back to weigh the mushrooms and bag them for two of the farm women, who were headed to the market to sell them.

Oyster mushrooms are 10% protein, which makes them an affordable cheap addition to the typical low protein Ghanaian diet. Millions of children in Africa die annually from 'kwashiorkor', a protein deficiency disease, so farmers are encouraged to grow mushrooms. So far, the children of the farm workers here and the kids at the school don't show any signs of having kwashiorkor disease so they must be eating oyster mushrooms with rice like Joyce is feeding me.

Vicki tells me Volta Farms hopes some volunteers will come in the near future and help them start a shiitake mushroom growing project. Shiitake mushrooms tend to grow on old hardwood tree logs that are plentiful in the jungle. This species of mushroom provide 18% protein and provide many nutritional benefits, like strengthening the immune systems of people who eat them regularly. Best of all, they take far less labor and water than oyster mushrooms. After they are bagged and cleaned, they will keep for three weeks, which is ten times longer than the shelf life of the oyster mushrooms.

After the chores are finished up I'm in for a real treat. Vicki takes me on a short walk to the market. The market is bustling and brimming with bright colors just like in online photos. (Just Google 'markets in Ghana' if you need a visual). Yes, there are flies everywhere, but once you accept that as a fact of life here, it's quite wonderful to experience one of these open markets with a guide like Vicki. As I said, she's such a friendly person, cheerfully chatting with everyone she knows as she introduces me as, 'Mandi-the-Yovo'.

I was able to find four yards of batik fabric with West African designs I really liked. Sadly, cheap imitation Chinese textile imports have wiped out three quarters of Ghana's once thriving textile industry. In the last two decades, over 25,000 Ghanaian textile laborers have become unemployed. To make matters worse, illegal Chinese copies of unique Ghanaian designs, that were originally printed using wax, are now imitated and smuggled into Ghana on a regular basis. Authentic Ghanaian logos, patents, and trademarks have been stolen by these illegal producers. Across the country, local market places are flooded with these imitation fabrics from China, making it almost impossible, even for experts, to find the true and authentic West

African cloth among all the illegal replicas. Sadly, these smuggled fabrics sell for considerably less, making them popular for Ghanaians who can't afford the real thing. We searched and searched for authentic Ghanaian fabric at all the display booths but in the end, it proved futile to find the real thing so the batik fabric I bought cost me only six cedis (like $5 CAD – at the time I travelled a cedis was worth about $.80 CAD).

Next, Vicki took me to a dressmaker who had me choose the dress styles I wanted. In total, I will have two custom made dresses ready for pickup in four days for the equivalent of $34.00 CAD. I also bought a new calling card for my cell phone and, just before we headed back to Volta Farms, Vicki bought a live chicken. I tried not to look at it as we walked home because I couldn't stop wondering how much of it was going to end up on my dinner plate. Joyce is still serving me huge portions of food and acts terribly affronted when I can't finish everything on my plate. Needless to say, I have a difficult time eating a chicken that had been enjoying its life just a couple of hours ago! (PS – luckily this one wasn't pink inside or out!)

Have I mentioned lizards yet? There are agama lizards everywhere and they freak me out. They're not cute and small like the little friendly geckos you see on vacation in Mexico. Oh no, these reptiles, with garish bright orange heads, are sometimes a foot long in the body. I'm completely creeped out by them. It is gross to walk into the bathroom and see one scurry away—just as horrifying as finding a big ugly rat sharing your home. I'm not even going to get into that!

And the bugs! Every day I see at least one new kind of bug. First, it was the giant centipedes and I do mean giant. They average about 25 centimeters (10 inches) in length, which is 24 centimeters too long for my liking. Then there are the jumping green leaf bugs that land on me instead of the thousands of jungle plants they could choose. Thank goodness, they are very tiny. Their insides are blue, a discovery I made after squishing one— accidentally of course.

Speaking of tiny, that's the size of the native mosquitoes here. They are miniature, silent versions of their highly annoying Canadian cousins, and their bites are just as itchy. Last but not least is my gruesome discovery of a huge flat spider species. How huge you ask? They are as big as my hand, which means they can go to the front of the line ahead of the orange-headed lizards for being the freakiest thing I've ever seen. Seriously, I would have to use a dinner plate to cover one of them. Even though they are not poisonous, I hope and pray I never have to deal with one in my bed or in my suitcase. On that note, it's very important that I briskly shake any clothes I'm about to put on because anything could be napping in them. OK, now I'm creeping myself out too much. (You'll find out later that I forgot to mention all this to my mom, I may have even told her that I don't really remember any bugs in Ghana…)

It's now day... I don't know as I'm not counting them anymore. I'm here for months, did you really think I was going to track every single day? And seriously, saying what day it is, well, it's filler so my story looks longer and uses up more pages and what do you care if it's day ten or twelve right now? Right!

Yesterday, whatever day that was, was a full day of tours around the Volta Region. I had a precarious start to my touring adventures, no thanks to Cheech. To say I'm not very happy with Cheech is a colossal understatement. Remember, he's contracted by 3W Volunteers to 'guide us' but the term must mean something different to him. He was supposed to pick me up and personally guide me to the place where I would join other volunteers for our next tours. Instead, I received a call from him instructing me to hitch a ride to the Ho trotro station and travel to Hohoe to rendezvous with him at the trotro station there. After a half hour ride from Volta Farms to the Ho trotro station in a new white farm truck, donated by an American church, I rode alone by trotro for the 45 kilometer (28 mile) trip to the city of Hohoe. En route, I received a second call from him, informing me he would be delayed. The new plan was for me to taxi from the Hohoe trotro station to a lodge that would be my accommodations for the next two days. There I would join the rest of the volunteers going on tours with Cheech.

How does a white girl from Alberta get a taxi in a trotro station when she doesn't speak a word of Ewe, the native language predominantly spoken in this region of Ghana? She doesn't. By now, I'm convinced the claims by Ghanaian Tourism that 'everyone speaks English' is quite an exaggeration. I wandered helplessly around the trotro station searching for someone who spoke English.

Despite this setback, I have to say though, that Ghanaian people are so sweet in general. There is a standard protocol used when greeting one another and virtually all Ghanaians say it in English. I follow it too, to show respect. It goes like this:

"Hello, how are you?"

"I am fine, thank you, and you?"

"I am also fine, thank you."

So even when I just need to ask a simple question to find out if a person can speak English, first we exchange this greeting. Of course, by now I understand that just because a Ghanaian can speak this greeting in perfect English does not mean they can actually converse in English.

My quest continued for more than thirty minutes until a young man pointed to his car and in garbled English, offered to drive me to the lodge. I must admit, I threw caution to the wind as I took him up on his offer. He seemed well intentioned so I just sat myself down in the passenger seat and crossed my fingers. My mom is going to freak when she reads this part! I promised her that we volunteers would never be left by ourselves. Thankfully, a few minutes later, we pulled up to the lodge and I immediately saw Deidre eating at an outdoor table. I thanked the young man at the wheel profusely for his kind deed, paid him and hopped out quickly as Deidre rushed over to hug me.

We were both so happy to jabber together for the rest of the evening while we hung out at the lodge with a number of other volunteers. The next morning, Cheech finally did what was in his job description and guided us to our first tour, the Monkey Sanctuary at Tafi Atome, located about 20 kilometers (12 miles) south of Hohoe. The road was the roughest I have been on, and considering the state of most roads I've traveled in Ghana, that means it barely qualified as a road. Ruts, presumably caused by runoff after rainstorms, had grown into deep crevices. Our driver calmly drove through them, causing the trotro to lean from side to side at precarious angles, depending on which two wheels sank the deepest. When I wasn't focused on trying to avoid being pitched into someone's lap as we bounced along, I noticed we were passing small villages with clusters of the poorest-of-the-poor type of mud-huts. It felt like we were being driven into Joseph Conrad's *Heart of Darkness*, all the more so when a river appeared to our right. No, it wasn't the Congo River but it could have been. The jungle was much denser here and the trees had almost doubled in size, creating the same sort of dark, damp, pungent smelling setting as in the aforementioned novel.

We finally exited the trotro and soon fell into line behind our designated sanctuary guide who promptly led us to a trailhead that would take us into the jungle. As we walked the humidity rose even higher, within five minutes our clothes were saturated

40

with perspiration. The trail was very rough and we had to be careful not to walk into huge spiders' webs. Bugs were everywhere.

After walking deep into the jungle for about fifteen minutes, our sanctuary guide began calling to the Mona monkeys, in monkey-language I presumed, to come down from the tree canopy above us so we could feed them. Although they are wild and free to come and go, these monkeys have stayed here in the sanctuary for over two hundred years where they are protected from hunters and poachers. I like the fact that income generated by this ecotourism is being used to expand the preservation of the forest. The locals believe these Mona monkeys are special messengers from a god and therefore they should be respected as if they are the human relatives of the village inhabitants. When a monkey dies, it is even given a funeral and burial equal to that of a human. These little black and white monkeys were playful, but very well behaved and daintily took bananas from our hands. Their good manners were a great relief to me because I knew some of them carried rabies and was all too aware I had not bothered to cough up the exorbitant price of $800.00 CAD for a rabies vaccination before my trip.

Next we traveled by trotro for about 40 kilometers (25 miles) northwest to our next tour destination, Wli Falls, nestled in the Agmasta Wildlife Sanctuary. They were spectacular—not massive like Niagara Falls but incredibly beautiful as they cascaded about 70 meters (77 yards) down a steep rock face into large, deep pools at the bottom. As we had walked along the trail to them, the dense jungle canopy above our heads had gradually opened up to reveal the falls, allowing the African sunlight to create reams of rainbows as it bounced off the moving prisms of thousands of water droplets. It was a spectacle of stunning beauty that had cameras clicking away non-stop.

We had to walk for half an hour to get to them, so like always, my clothes remained soaked in sweat. It seems as if this is just an unpleasant fact of life here. I'm happy to report that the plunging waterfalls filled the air with cool mist and made this place the only refreshing environment I've experienced in Ghana. Before people from our group waded into the water for a cool swim, our local guide thoroughly explained the potentially fatal risks of swimming too close to the base of the falls where the thunderous waters pounded with deadly force into the deep pools. Other groups of people were already in the water, including some adrenaline junkies who tempted fate by swimming right under the falls despite the verbal warnings and large signs everywhere that many people drown doing just that.

Our last tour, also situated in the Agmasta Wildlife Sanctuary, began within walking distance of the Wli Falls. Once our group reconvened, we took a hiking trail that led us up a long, horribly hot ascent to the summit of Mount Afadjato. The temperature climbed to 40 degrees Celsius (104 degrees Fahrenheit), which feels like a million degrees, as we hiked up a forty degree incline to the 915 meter (1,000 yards) high summit. Now, I'm no stranger to hiking up mountains—my parents were always dragging my siblings and me up steep hiking trails in the mountains of Banff or Jasper Park, to reach some of the most breathtaking vistas in all of Canada. I had said yes to this tour because Mount Afadjato looked like an easy, sissy climb when I checked it out online, but the heat and humidity turned it into a hellish extreme sporting event. By the time we reached the top, everyone was staggering with exhaustion and I didn't think any of us would give a hoot about the scenery. Luckily, I was wrong. You'd have to be dead not to be enthralled by the stunning, incredibly breathtaking views from the top. Amazing, jaw dropping, sensational, phenomenal... in other words, it was well worth the suffering. However, that being said, one hike up Mount Afadjato shall suffice in my lifetime. Note to guides: Instead of leading us right back to the parking lot, it would've been nice to take us to the Wli Falls AFTER our grueling hike up Mt. Afadjato so the refreshing cool misty air could resuscitate us all... yes?

It is mid-July now, and I am very excited to tell you my good news. I'm leaving Volta Farms and moving to The Last Hope Children's Home in Anagonyigba, where Deidre is volunteering. I couldn't be happier. During the recent tours we went on together, Deirdre was sharing how wonderful it was to be so involved in the daily lives of the children. When I told her how boring my stay at Volta Farms had turned out to be, she offered to talk to the operating directors of The Last Hope Children's

Home to see if I could switch my volunteer term to there, so I could join her. I asked Cheech if I could move, and he vehemently refused my request, telling me that because my money had been given to Volta Farms, I had no choice but to stay there for the duration of my term. That left me very disappointed, so imagine my surprise when he called this morning to give me permission to pack up and leave. He sounded quite angry but I don't care, I am already packed and ready to go. Soon, I will be hitching a ride by farm truck, to the trotro station in Ho. Goodbye biting ants, smelly ducks, weird rodents, dead snails, and mammoth sized meals!

Now I'm in Africa living my dream, helping little brown-skinned children who have flies buzzing around their sweet faces. They are all a wee bit potbellied from lack of adequate ideal nutrition but they're much cleaner than the sad faces on television that mesmerized me throughout my childhood.

Deidre met me at the trotro station in Anagonyigba and we chatted happily, as we set out on the one kilometer walk to the Last Hope Children's Home. In Anagonyigba, there are no nicely planned city blocks and streets. Roads and paths are strewn about willy-nilly, creating a confusing maze, and I tried my best to memorize the route as we went along. Deidre reassured me that I would not have to do this route solo until I could confidently navigate it on my own. I'm thinking to myself that will hopefully not be anytime soon.

The Last Hope Children's Home is a faded, U-shaped building. In the front, it has a play area of hard packed red dirt, which has the odd patch of trampled and worn out grass defiantly surviving under the relentless sun. The front entrance has matching, well-tended, small flowerbeds on either side of it, and several large leafed trees offer spotty shade around the property.

The compound looked abandoned except for two boys. It seemed there was an orange causing quite a kerfuffle between them. The orange was currently in the hands of the older boy. Though unable to match the strength of the older boy, the much smaller boy was lightning fast. He relentlessly pursued the older boy, trying desperately to gain possession of the orange. Alas, strength won in the end, and the smaller boy, who looked no older than three or four, burst into tears when he was finally defeated.

I, of course, instinctively hurried over to lift him into my arms. He settled down immediately, rubbing his little button nose against my top. Then he looked up at me—two large, round, black eyes shining brightly in an adorable upturned pudgy brown face. He was quite possibly, the cutest child I had ever laid eyes on and within one beat, my heart expanded and my universe shifted. It was love at first sight. A few minutes later, when I set him down, he quickly grabbed the soda I had placed on a table moments before, and toasted our new friendship by immediately gulping it down in record time. As I caught him at it, he flashed a sweet smile laced with so much innocent confidence in my goodwill that an intangible link grew between us. His entire petite personhood then shot me an unmistakable message—I pick you. Please say yes!

Here, the vision I've carried from my childhood became connected to the present moment—taking shape and form right there in front of my eyes. I felt an invisible cord pulling me into connection with this skinny little boy, whose eyes dazzle as bright as the brightest stars that blanket the night skies here. I was face to face, in Africa, having a World-Vision moment of my own. I know that sounds uncharacteristically mushy but that's the only way I can describe it.

In the meantime, Effia, one of the two operating directors running The Last Hope Children's Home, had come out to meet us. I'm 5 ft. 4 inches tall and maybe on the slim side of average weight. Effia is the same height but she is easily double my weight. She is a very stocky, solidly built woman with big hips and a very ample bosom. She extended a warm welcome to me, but as she shook my hand I almost winced. She has thick, strong hands that would be masculine looking except for her manicured painted nails. Effia's face is round, her skin looks like smooth, shiny dark chocolate, and she has the typical Ghanaian lovely full lips and dark eyes with her hair braided into perfect, glossy cornrows.

Effia's clothes looked as if they had been painted on, they were so tight her very large bosom looked alarmingly close to bursting the restrictions of a shirt sized for a much smaller woman. I have no idea how she got into jeans as tight as the pair she was wearing and it is beyond my comprehension why anyone in their right mind, would want to be trapped in such tight clothes in this extreme heat and humidity.

Effia offered to give me a tour of the home and property. The children were still attending private school, she explained. I didn't see where the older boy who had won the battle over the orange had gone but a certain adorable pudgy faced little boy now shadowed me everywhere I went. Effia took no notice of him except to tell me his name; Atsu (pronounced like a sneeze 'A-choo').

The director's office is situated to the left of the front entrance of the Last Hope Children's Home, which, by the way, is called Last Hope by everyone here so from now on, that's what I'll call it too. The office is also the designated First Aid room. We went through it to a smallish room where the youngest boys slept. It shared a wall with an unoccupied nursery. Passing through the small nursery took us to another small room. This is where the other operating director, a woman named Selorm whom I hadn't met yet, slept.

Her room is the last of the rooms that run down the left side of the building so from there we turned right and entered a small kitchen. It serviced the largest area in the home, a big room called the Common Room. This room contains four long tables surrounded by plastic chairs, like those used as patio furniture in Canada. Effia told me this is where the children have their meals. At the back of this room, close to the kitchen, there is a smaller table covered with a plastic checkered tablecloth. This is where the volunteers are to sit at mealtimes, Effia informed me. She went on to say that, the children are strictly forbidden to go near us volunteers during our mealtimes.

Along the right side of the Common Room, there is a large, walk-in food storage area and a freezer. There are also two doors along the far right wall. The door closest to the food storage area took us into the boys' dorm. The other one led into the girls' dorm. Each dorm contains many three-tiered bunk beds placed close together. Together these two dorms fill all the space along the right side of Last Hope. That leaves just one more room, a small, single bedroom that runs along the front wall of Last Hope. Inside, it is bare except for a single bed and a narrow wall shelf. I noticed it had one door leading directly outside to the front entrance of Last Hope. The other door leads back into the Common Room. Surprisingly, Deidre opts to sleep here, foregoing the modern conveniences that the volunteer house has to offer.

That ended my tour of Last Hope and next Effia and I (and my little brown shadow, Atsu) walked around the rest of the compound. Across from the dorms, on the right side of the compound, there were outdoor shower stalls and outhouses. Beside this, Effia pointed out a tap that was their only source of water. She was quick to warn me that foreigners should never drink this water. "It will make you very sick," she told me, "Only we locals can drink it."

To the right of the water tap, facing the road was a building that used to house a music school. "We don't own it," Effia said to me, "I don't know what they are going to use it for in the future". Behind the old music school, clothes hung out to dry on long lines. In the back right corner of the compound, there was a crude structure with long poles holding up its roof. The floor was dirt and an assortment of random church pews were set up. It is a church, which is not part of Last Hope, Effia explained to me. She didn't elaborate as she continued my tour.

Next, we passed some chickens in their coop and some goats that lay dozing in the shady corner of their pen. This completed my tour and next, Effia introduced me to Jeremy. He is a very charismatic six foot tall, eighteen year old boy, who is the oldest child at the Last Hope Children's Home. Jeremy could be a male model he is so good looking. He has an athletic build, a well-defined strong jaw, perfectly shaped eyebrows, almond shaped, deep black eyes and wide, full lips. His beautiful white teeth and catalogue perfect ear-to-ear warm smile belong in a toothpaste advertisement. He has black, short-cropped corkscrew hair brushed into a fluffy short curly mat; every inch of him is well groomed from top to bottom. He explained to me, in the best English I've heard so far, that the rest of the children call him 'Dada' because he is the oldest male living here. He shares the nighttime supervision role with the senior operational director, Selorm, and Deidre.

Reluctantly, it was time for Deidre and me to continue on to the volunteer house. After Deidre led me through another haphazard maze of paths, we arrived. Half a dozen volunteers already occupy the house but it accommodates up to ten people, so there is room for me. The living conditions are better than I expected. There is a little porch attached out front, the living room has furniture, and the kitchen has a fridge to store cold drinks. The floors are tiled throughout the house and the bathroom even has a modern flush toilet next to the cold-water-only shower stall. I chose a single bed in the four-bed girl's room and immediately put up mosquito netting around it so I could look forward to a relatively bug-free sleep.

Overall, these are the most luxurious living conditions I've seen on my trip so far but as nice as it is here, I know I will only use this house for a place to sleep. I want all my waking hours to be spent with the children of Last Hope. I'm so anxious to be busy and stay busy after the low-key sojourn I've just had at Volta Farms.

The next day I meet the senior director of The Last Hope Children's Home, Selorm. She is quite rotund and while only 5'5 feet tall, she's one of those people whose presence takes up big space in a room. Selorm has noticeably chubby cheeks separated by a flat wide nose. Her eyes are pure coal black and her plump hands have big knuckled fingers. She has a plethora of small, tightly braided hair extensions pulled back into a huge, thick ponytail by a bright, multicolored scarf and her extensions all swing and bounce, accentuating her movements.

Selorm gave me a very hospitable welcome but there is a matronly assertiveness to her. Effia, on the other hand is more easygoing and approachable, and so far, she's the one we work alongside the most. Also, both of them speak English, although they speak it with a very heavy Ghanaian accent. Accents or no accents, being able to converse in English makes life here a lot easier than at Volta Farms.

Here at Last Hope, I am happy and busy as I do what I love to do—lend a hand where help is needed and with forty-two children housed here, it's needed. Every morning the children shower and pomade themselves until their skin is glossy and moist. Pomade is made locally in Ghana from a mixture containing shea butter and bees wax. Without the protective coating and moisture it provides, their skin would turn gray. The only gray-skinned people I've seen here were homeless street beggars in Accra who obviously can't afford Pomade.

I'm impressed with how tidy the children keep their hair all the time. Deidre told me Selorm is a former hairdresser and she makes sure the girls' hair is always braided into perfectly aligned, tight cornrows. The boys' hair is regularly cut very short and Selorm insists they brush it energetically until it becomes soft and bushy.

After the children take their morning shower they eat breakfast, which the older girls help cook and serve. Their typical breakfast could be oblayo (maize porridge) or rice porridge (called rice water here), served with sugar tea or milo (an unsweetened, much diluted cocoa drink). Meals are brought into the hall and the children line up around the tables. Then the food is portioned out and the children are called up one by one (their names are on the bottom of the bowls) to receive their food. They eat at the tables in the hall. The smaller children eat on stools with their bowls on their laps. After meals, the girls of all ages work together washing and drying the dishes, then the school-aged children change into their uniforms, brush their teeth, and file past Effia and Selorm for inspection before walking to school.

On weekdays, Last Hope runs a preschool program and the older children go to a private school in Anagonyigba. Their education is funded by donations. They won't get to eat again until after three in the afternoon, when school finishes. This after-school meal is considered their lunch and spaghetti with tomato sauce is almost always served. The dinner menu alternates between banku (fermented corn & cassava dough added to a soup broth), waakye (rice and beans), okra soup or redred (bean stew with fried plantain).

I haven't seen them offer much in the way of fresh fruits and vegetables since I've been here, but there is plenty of food. It's offensive to leave anything on one's plate but the average-sized food portions make it very manageable to finish a whole meal.

We volunteers are served our lunch at midday. I can't help feeling guilty about getting this meal hours ahead of the children.

They are the ones with growing bodies and I wish they could be the ones eating now instead of waiting three more hours. It seems like such a long time for them to go without food.

The food fare we are served is starchy, but it is delicious because Selorm is an incredible cook. We never have to wait for our meals, as she seems to take pride in having all our meals prepared and served to us punctually.

As I previously mentioned, the children can drink the water from the tap that is outside beside the shower stalls. We foreigners must avoid it and buy safe water or risk suffering the ill effects of parasites. I try not to think about the water source used in cooking our meals. It's almost impossible to avoid picking up some sort of parasite during long visits to any West African country. Most globetrotters know and accept that treatment for parasites is a no-brainer upon returning home.

While the kids have been away at school this week, Deidre, another volunteer named Mahault and I have been busy painting the exterior of Last Hope. We've used bright colors to add some new life to the drab looking walls. We also had all the children and the operating directors add their handprints to the front exterior wall that faces the street. Everyone had great fun doing it and when it was finished, we were all pleased with the decorative effect.

After the children return from school and eat their after-school meal, we help them with their homework, play games with them, and teach them better hygiene. During my trips around Ghana, it seems a common practice for children to just squat and pee or poop wherever...whenever! Here at Last Hope, the first thing they must learn is the fine art of using an outhouse. Every trip to the outhouse must be followed with a thorough washing of their hands. With forty-two children, most of them young, we are constantly helping them to master these two routines to ensure better hygiene for everyone.

We also make sure they brush their teeth. At first, the children ate the toothpaste we provided them as if it was candy, now we load it on their toothbrushes for them and keep all the toothpaste locked in the supply cupboard. Too funny! In the evening, all the children shower again and then we read them stories and tuck them into bed for the night.

I know that it is impossible for just two people, Effia and Selorm, to match the same level of help and attention that we volunteers provide the children. How does this place run without volunteers? The children must be left to fend for themselves quite often, and that thought saddens me deeply. Except for Jeremy and a handful of teenage boys, most of the children are young. There is no program in place to guarantee volunteers will be here every week throughout the year. When I asked Effia how they coped during the times volunteers were not here to help, she just shrugged her shoulders and said, "We manage." Her tone definitely indicated that was the extent of her answer and the subject was closed.

Yesterday was Saturday, the official weekly laundry day and Last Hope turned into a miniature, sudsy work camp. All the children wash their own clothes with military precision. Even the younger ones do it with assistance from the older children.

Everyone takes their turn at one of the many large buckets filled with water. Surprisingly, there are no washboards used, even though they were as common in Africa, as in Europe, before the invention of the washing machine. Anyway, the kids just use a bar of hard soap and their little brown hands scrub away as if their lives depend on it. Every garment is washed vigorously twice, then it's double rinsed before it is twisted over and over again to force out the excess water. The lines stretched out behind the old music school building are soon filled to capacity with wet clothes. I've never seen hand-scrubbed clothes turn out so clean.

In the evenings, after we say our goodbyes to Deidre and the children, Mahault and I walk back to the volunteer house along the paths and across the plank bridges. It is always pitch black so we go slowly. The jungle night gobbles up the light from our small flashlights, like a starving piranha. After we arrive, we shower, have cool drinks, play cards and talk or listen to music until it is time to go to sleep. It's a simple routine and life is easier now that my body has adapted, somewhat, to the incredible heat and humidity.

Today, I learned the story of two of the boys. The government workers from Ghanaian Social Welfare rescued them, age five and three years old and brought them to Last Hope. Their father had sold them into slavery, to a fisherman, in exchange for a cow. The two brothers spent all the daylight hours in the highly polluted waters of Lake Volta, untangling fishing nets. It seems ludicrous to me that any child can spend twelve hours in the water day after day. I also learned that many of these child-slaves drown. I can't even fathom how these two very young boys, had survived this long. Compared to what their life had become at the hands of the fishermen, Last Hope was a much safer haven for them.

I had no idea that when I came to Last Hope, I would need to take so many children back and forth to the hospital in Anagonyigba. Malaria is what necessitates all these trips. There are no screens on any of the doors or windows in Last Hope and mosquitoes feast repeatedly on the children, giving them malaria. This happens on a regular basis so every week I shepherd children with malaria back and forth to the hospital for treatment.

This week, the operating directors accepted two new children into their care at Last Hope. They are siblings and are the skinniest kids I've ever seen. I am able to count their ribs and their potbellies protrude so far, you almost expect the skin to split wide open at any given moment. The girl, Lovely, is six and the little boy, Heaven, is just three. Such sweet names for such forlorn little children.

This is their story: their mother died when Heaven was an infant. The father could not care for his young children, so he took them to live with his parents. The grandparents tried to care for them, but both of the children became chronically ill. As time went on, Lovely and Heaven became very, very sick. That is why their grandparents have handed them over to Last Hope. They hope their grandchildren will now receive the medical help they each so desperately need.

Both these kids were extremely weak when they arrived, so we immediately offered them some food. Lovely ate a little bit on her own, but the little boy, Heaven, had no interest in food at all. I tried to hand-feed him bits of scrambled eggs but he remained lethargic and disinterested. I did manage to get a couple of spoonfuls of soup into him sporadically for the rest of the day, but that was all. Attempts to feed him the next morning were equally unsuccessful, but Lovely managed to eat a little more food at breakfast.

Selorm and Effia asked Deidre and I to take my little brown shadow, Atsu, and these two very sick little ones to the hospital. The operating directors have a policy that all new arrivals must be tested for malaria and HIV. Atsu had arrived only days before I did and hadn't been to the hospital yet.

I think I know why the operating directors instruct volunteers to do these hospital trips. None of the three children owned a mandatory national medical card, and without one they would not receive any treatment. Needless to say, Deidre and I could not let that happen, so we forked over the money to buy medical cards for all three children. Are you reading between the lines on why the volunteers take the children for treatment?

When it was time for blood tests, the two siblings were tested first. I think they were so sick they couldn't muster the strength to react much when their little fingers were pricked. I had Atsu on my lap and as soon as his finger was pricked, he went into a frenzied panic. He thrashed about, twisting and turning and squirming like a miniature Olympic wrestler trying to prevent a take down. By the time we calmed him, the blood on his finger had already dried and he needed to be pricked a second time so a couple of blood drops could be collected in a tiny glass vial.

The doctor picked up a contaminated lancet from out of the used pile and proceeded to prick Atsu's finger with it. I threw a fit! It was impossible for the doctor to know if the lancet he just reused was the same one he originally used to prick Atsu's finger. It could just as easily have been a lancet used on Heaven or Lovely. All three used lancets looked identical. We didn't know yet, if any of these three children were going to test positive for HIV and I was furious about this doctor's carelessness. We are in Ghana, where a quarter of a million people are infected with HIV. I was in a state of utter shock and rage.

After Atsu's blood was finally collected, we all sat down in the waiting room. We could not leave until we knew the results of the children's blood tests. After about thirty minutes, the doctor came out and ushered us into his private office. I knew something wasn't right and began to feel nervous. He confirmed that both Lovely and Heaven had tested HIV positive so he needed to give each of them a thorough physical examination. His demeanor became more and more serious while he worked.

When he was finished examining Heaven and Lovely, he stepped back and told Deidre and I that the disease was very advanced in both of them. He went on to tell us that because neither child had received any prior treatment for their HIV; his prognosis was that the illness would now be fatal for both of them.

This devastating news hit me like a tidal wave. I can't even find the words to describe how horrific it was to hear this death sentence pronounced on two children sitting right in front of me. On top of that, my mind spun in a frenzy of worry as I digested the possibility that Atsu could now be infected with HIV because of this doctor's sloppy, non-sterile actions with a contaminated lancet.

I think the doctor had ushered us into the privacy of his office because he knew he had been careless. I glared at him and made it very clear that we would be returning in twelve days to retest Atsu for HIV, using the RNA blood plasma test. I specifically asked for this test because I knew it would detect the presence of HIV much sooner than the standard, quick, antibodies test. I stated emphatically that we would keep retesting Atsu until he was safely through the window period of possible HIV infection. And I growled that we wouldn't be paying for any of these tests. He could damn well cover the costs out of his own pocket.

Deidre and I returned to Last Hope with heavy hearts. We had two seriously ill HIV positive children and one more young life now placed in jeopardy. Lovely took the medications the hospital gave us and she remained stable, but over the next few days, the situation with Heaven, the three year old, quickly became worse. He was a gravely ill little boy. We had to hold him down and force medication into his little mouth because he refused to take it on his own. He would not or could not eat and he went downhill very quickly.

Honestly, we did everything we could for poor little Heaven. We shuffled him to and from the hospital for daily intravenous drugs and fluids. All the volunteers held him as much as possible. And then, just like that, he was gone....

This is so heart-wrenching. I'm in a third world country and the space between life and death is so much narrower than in a modern country like Canada. I still can't believe a little life I've held in my arms has perished.

I have so many emotions pouring through me at the same time. Part of me is infuriated. Why did his grandparents wait so long to bring him here? Why didn't someone suspect HIV a long time ago when he first got sick and didn't recover? And, to make matters worse, Effia and Selorm act detached and unemotional. They've treated his death as if it were an everyday occurrence here at Last Hope, so part of me is mad at them for appearing so untouched by his death. Maybe you have to have a hardened heart to survive life in Ghana.

I ache with grief yet I feel completely hollow at the same time. It's easy to say life isn't fair, but it is excruciating to witness life's unfairness when a little three year old dies because his family could not afford to get him the medical help he needed.

There is also something else that is really troubling me lately about Selorm and Effia. It's the way in which they discipline the children. Both of them are extremely strict disciplinarians. I do understand the necessity of having rules to keep things running smoothly when there are this many children living under one roof. I totally get that, but it is the methods of their discipline that unsettle me more and more each time I witness it.

The other day, a boy walking past me, failed to say hello to me. Selorm announced he had been discourteous to me. It was one of her rules that all the children had to greet a volunteer politely if our paths crossed on the property. Selorm made him stand up on a table outside, under the blistering hot sun, for an hour. He was not allowed to move a muscle. (Even I could not do that—stand there absolutely motionless for an hour in this heat!) My face must have shown my consternation because Selorm gave me a glare, that made me bite my tongue from commenting—and as I'm sure you have gathered, I have a tendency to speak my mind. Her glare was something else. In that moment, it was as if an invisible door had opened, briefly revealing a much darker side of her. Just as suddenly, it was over, but the momentary change in her demeanor startled me. I can't explain this very well...you'd have to be here in person to experience it for yourself. (Note: Not recommended—I mean why would you put yourself through that?)

Sometimes the children are caned for breaking rules. In a family unit, the father would take this role, therefore Jeremy is summoned to do the caning because he is the oldest male here. It's shocking to see the number of permanent discolored marks some of the children have on their backs, which tells me caning is a frequent form of punishment here at Last Hope.

It's very difficult to watch all this happen right in front of my eyes, but as a foreigner, I have to be aware of the fine line I must walk. I know I must not interfere with anyone's actions that stem from the culture or customs practiced here in Ghana. It's tough though, to see these forms of discipline used on the children and not be able to speak up on their behalf. After Selorm's dark glare, I had a strange feeling that I just might make it worse for a child if I were to interfere. Effia flashed me the same type of dark, silencing glare when she gave Jeremy orders, right in front of me, to cane another child for breaking a rule. Clearly, both operating directors would prefer for me to mind my own business.

I talk over my concerns with the other volunteers. They all agreed and disclosed that they too receive these types of dark glares when they witness Effia or Selorm disciplining the children in these ways. At least that tells me I'm not being singled out to mind my own business.

Generally speaking the directors have been great hosts; mostly warm and hospitable except when children disobey their rules. I'm constantly aware how vulnerable these kids are because they have nowhere else to go. If they are not cared for here, or somewhere else, most will end up as statistics in some form of child slavery within Ghana. They will live harsh and short lives

62

as laborers in the fishing and agricultural sectors or worse, be exploited in the child sex trade industry.

Dealing with serious illnesses and death has made me feel extremely protective towards these children. Right now, their vulnerability is first and foremost on my mind. I'm tough enough to ride this out. I knew it wouldn't be all sunshine, lollipops, and roses here. But it is very frustrating.

To take my mind off the children, I think back to a new piece of information I just learned about. Atsu's name isn't actually Atsu. How strange is that? The medical card he was issued states his name is actually Caleb Lebbih. When I asked Selorm and Effia at Last Hope questions about his name, they told me Atsu is a common Ghanaian nickname for the second-born twin so that is why they use it. They didn't have any information about his twin. Atsu has a real knack for learning English and he understood me when I asked him if I should call him Caleb. My adorable little brown shadow said, "No, my name is Atsu!" So that's that, my brown shadow wants to be named after a sneeze.

I know we aren't counting days anymore, but plenty of them have passed by. Last Monday, (really I could have said any day of the week, but Monday sounded about right), Deidre, Jeremy and I took little Atsu to the hospital in Anagonyigba to be circumcised. He has stolen my heart and become my little brown shadow from the moment I arrived at The Last Hope. Thus far I don't know much about him, but slowly I am gathering bits of information and putting his story together. A couple of days before I came here to Last Hope, Atsu had been dropped off here by his grandfather. Apparently, his grandparents were too poor to take care of him anymore. The poor little fellow did not comprehend that he would now be living here permanently. He waited at the gate from morning until night, expecting his grandfather to return for him. He bonded quite well with Deidre, but for some strange reason, since the first moment I laid eyes on him, he has stayed close by my side. The operating directors have been very lenient about allowing him to follow me around. That is why I refer to him as my little brown shadow. We are inseparable.

Effia and Selorm told me Atsu is just three years old, and refuses to sleep in the small bedroom designated for the younger boys, or in the older boys' dorm. The situation was solved when a six-year-old girl named Peace took him with her at bedtime and let him sleep on a ground mat beside her bottom bunk bed. No one knows why she did this. She is developmentally slow and very sweet and Atsu appears very content with this arrangement, so the directors have allowed him to continue to sleep beside Peace in the girls' dorm. Each night when I read stories to the girls at bedtime, they all accept that Atsu gets to curl up in my lap. Perhaps they remember what it was like to be afraid and uncertain when they first arrived here.

On Monday, Deidre and I had to accompany Jeremy and little Atsu to the Anagonyigba Hospital. The operating directors have talked us into taking Atsu to be circumcised for cultural reasons. Circumcision is a custom for all Ghanaian males, usually done at birth or shortly thereafter. An uncircumcised man will never be accepted for marriage. No one can tell me why Atsu was not circumcised at birth so the decision is made to take him to the hospital.

Jeremy accompanied Atsu into a small medical procedure room just down the hall from the waiting room where Deidre and I had to stay as women are not allowed to be present during a circumcision. A Cuban doctor and three male aids crowded into the tiny room. I wondered why it took so many medical personnel to circumcise such a little boy. To our horror, Atsu began to scream and shriek hysterically. Deidre and I looked at each other, stunned as we both came to the same realization. The doctors weren't using any form of anesthetic. The male aids must have been holding down Atsu while his foreskin was being cut off. As the procedure continued so did his screaming. The only time there were brief moments of silence was when Atsu had to pause to refill his small lungs. Even with the treatment room door closed, his screams penetrated the thin walls and filled the hallway and waiting room where Deidre and I had to stay.

Time seemed to drag as if every second had an anchor chained to it. Atsu's misery continued. When he became too hoarse to scream anymore, he began to sob loudly through the last minutes of his torment. After what felt like a decade, Jeremy finally carried him back to Deidre and I. Atsu's brown face had paled considerably and snot ran from his nose. His little chest heaved and his short hair and small torso were soaked with sweat.

I took Atsu from Jeremy and he buried his little dark head into my chest, sobbing quietly now—completely spent. I heard a bewildered, forlorn, abandoned little heart speaking volumes through those sobs and I couldn't imagine what his thoughts contained. It seemed a small thing to ignore my aching arms and the relentless heat while carrying him the entire three kilometers (2 miles) back to Last Hope. Along the way, we stopped and bought him a cold soda. He sipped and hiccupped his way through it before pressing his little face into my chest again for the remainder of our walk back to Last Hope.

Incredibly, three days later we had to take him to another hospital to have the procedure corrected. How can a doctor screw up a circumcision? I was heartsick, knowing little Atsu would be cut and stitched again without any type of freezing. He started screaming as soon as he saw the 'white-coats' approaching and who could blame him?

When Selorm and Effia discussed having Atsu circumcised, they left out the part that the procedure is typically done without any type of freezing. We wouldn't put a family pet through what Atsu has had to experience. It would be considered a travesty of law— an act of immoral cruelty, the type that spawns media storms with thousands of people screaming for the guilty party to be tossed in jail and the key thrown away.

But I have to remember that I am in Ghana, a third world country where a little boy's screams and shrieks are considered the norm while an important custom is followed. Customs are the cultural glue that holds social and familial relationships together, even if it means putting a three-year-old through hell twice. The sounds of this torturous procedure have twice coated the inside of my brain. When I recollect this memory, Atsu's screams still reverberate through my mind and my whole body remembers how it felt that day. Some memories remain with a person forever.

Here in Ghana, no antibiotic creams or medications are dispensed for post-circumcision care. At Last Hope, there is no pure water to keep the surgery site clean. After each of his trips to the hospital, Deidre and I bought an antibiotic cream for Atsu and so far, he has avoided infection. That in itself seems miraculous considering the lower level of hygiene practiced here and the impure water used to clean him.

I can't tell you how much my heart expands with more and more love for this precious little boy. When Atsu crawls into my lap at story time, I wish I could keep him there forever and stave off anything that attempts to add to his suffering or fear or loneliness. Along with Atsu's recovery, there is another miracle also unfolding here. Lovely, the little six-year-old girl sick with HIV seems to be rallying and getting stronger. She's very good about taking her medicine which helps. She is a fussy eater though, so we all concentrated our efforts to figure out which foods Lovely liked enough to eat in bigger portions. We have a list of them now, and Lovely is gradually putting on weight and gaining energy. I cannot imagine what she's going through, and even though there is a language barrier, all of us volunteers try to comfort her whenever we can. Still, she remains a very sad, unsmiling little girl, who is undoubtedly trying to cope with the death of her younger sibling and her new surroundings here at Last Hope.

These past weeks have provided me with indelible memories that I will no doubt carry for the rest of my life; one child is dead, one child is fighting to survive advanced HIV, and it took two attempts to cut off a little boy's foreskin correctly. There we have it—the reality of archaic healthcare in Ghana has reared its head in many ways. Ghana may be inching its way out of a third world archetype, but its healthcare system clearly indicates that as a country, it has a lot to do before it can truly distance itself from that label.

Countless days later (because we stopped counting way back remember?), I can't believe I'm sitting back in the Accra Airport waiting for my return flight home. The days in Ghana flew by. We volunteers went on another tour guided by Cheech, which eventually imploded into the dramatic ending of our entire group's relationship with him. We went to the town of Elmina near Cape Coast and toured the Elmina Slave Castle, founded by the Portuguese in the 1480's. It is an enormous white structure with a red tiled roof and is majestically situated on top of a hill. From a distance, its distinctive roof makes it look so attractive; it could be mistaken for an old Mediterranean resort. I wish that was true. In its day, it was a trading post for gold and ivory and essentially a big box store like Walmart™ or Target™, that offered the most sought after commodity in The New World— slaves. Sadly, despite its striking architecture, thousands of slaves were imprisoned in its dungeons. There they languished until they were sold to slave traders and shipped to Europe.

Slavery was a cruel fate for anyone to face, and among the horrific stories the castle guide shared with us, it was the extreme abuses suffered by the females that made my stomach turn the most. If female prisoners refused to be available to their jailers to be gang-raped, they were then chained to massive steel balls located in the center of the castle's courtyard. There, they were left to suffer a slow and excruciating death in the burning African sun.

It was interesting to note that active slavery was commonly practiced amongst Africans long before the Europeans arrived. Our tour ended in a small musty cell that had a door called 'The Door of No Return'. Once slaves walked through it, they would emerge onto planks leading straight into the cargo holds of ships ready to sail back to Europe. There were fresh flowers, wreaths and mementos stacked up against this door—tributes to the untold numbers of human beings who had passed through 'The Door of No Return'. It was an incredibly sobering experience to be there.

For our return trip back to Anagonyigba, Cheech hired a trotro we came upon in a street in the town of Elmina. Then, he quickly sent us on our way without accompanying us back to

Anagonyigba, (again!), as he should have. His job responsibilities were clearly stated in the information given to us by his employer, 3W Volunteers. This was now the second or third time he had done this to our group. Our trotro driver was either drunk or high and he kept nodding off at the wheel. We all badgered him to stop and let us out. I stopped counting how many times our trotro swerved erratically or how often we drove with half the trotro in the ditch, narrowly missing abandoned cars. I'm positive he also managed to drive through every pothole too.

Needless to say, we made it back in one piece, but we were all furious with Cheech. Speaking for the group, I called him on my cell and demanded he return all of the remaining funds we had given him for the rest of our pre-booked tours. Eventually, we volunteers all received refunds and those of us at Last Hope put that money to good use during our last two weeks. Between all of us, we collectively purchased a lot for the children. We bought them more eating utensils so that sharing was no longer necessary. We made sure every child had flip-flops or shoes to wear. We supplied medical cards for all the children who needed them. A TV, DVD player, and educational DVD's were also purchased for the children. We had a fan installed in the Common Room and we installed screens on all the windows and doors of Last Hope. The screens have kept the mosquitoes at bay and there has been a noticeable decline in the incidences of malaria since we installed them.

Deidre left a week before I did, and I found my last days hard without her. Before she left, we decided to use some of our refunded money to pay for a trip to Wli Falls for all the children. It took a lot of organizing to coordinate enough trotros, and buy food and drinks for this special outing. The excitement grew more and more palpable as the big day arrived. Remember, visitors to Wli Falls have to walk a jungle trail to where they are located. I was continually amazed how effortlessly the older children carried everything we had brought with us, the Ghanaian way—on their heads. It was quite remarkable to see them balance their loads with grace and ease, while they walked over tree roots and avoided huge spider webs on the trail. Everyone had oodles of fun at the falls and it felt much more rewarding to use some of my money to make this happen for the children, instead of putting my life on the line riding in one of Cheech's hired trotros. And little six-year-old Lovely, the girl who arrived at Last Hope so sick with HIV, is now smiling. Oh my goodness, there is no way I will ever forget her first smile. She lit up the room with one of the most beautiful smiles I've ever seen—a smile that radiated through her dancing eyes, reflecting how perky she now feels. She's a fighter and demonstrates tenacity and strength each day to stay among the living, despite her serious illness. It is very hard to leave such an amazing, heroic little girl.

Atsu tested negative for HIV after that incompetent doctor pricked his finger with a contaminated lancet. I could have danced my way to the moon and back when I received the results of his HIV tests. Great news like this needs to be celebrated, especially after the tough emotional period before and after Heaven's death, the constant worry about Lovely's battle with HIV and the long worrisome wait for Atsu's blood test results. Atsu and I have been inseparable throughout my stay. He and I share an inexplicable bond that has deepened with each passing day. He's turned into a little geyser of affection and endless delightful smiles. He's very talkative, sociable and is quick to learn English. He easily shares with other kids and anytime he receives something, he quickly gives the giver a hug and says thank you.

However, yesterday, he was inconsolable. Tears flowed from his beautiful big brown eyes as I packed up my things. Atsu's tears spoke volumes to me about being abandoned and betrayed once again by an adult he loves. Even though I have done my best to assure him I will return, he has reverted back to the forlorn, sad little boy he was when he was dropped off here by his grandfather. We were both dreading this morning and it was pure hell to watch him cry hysterically as I climbed into a trotro to travel to the airport in Accra.

My recent experiences have shown me that the margin between happiness and grief can be very narrow. One's experiences can shift back and forth between the two much more frequently here in Ghana. In this hot and humid climate, all jungle plants grow rapidly—as does happiness and grief, hope and sorrow, comfort and pain. Nothing seems to stay the same.

Mosquitoes bring troubling malaria, but a fix like simple screens make a big difference. The Last Hope Children's Home offers care and a place to call home for many beautiful brown-faced children, but caning leaves scars on their little brown backs. Medicine can lengthen the lifespan of children with HIV, but poverty meant HIV brought death to frail little three-year-old Heaven. Medicine and better food brought back the light in Lovely's eyes, but those eyes also cry because she misses her dead little brother. Today, while I wait for my flight back to Canada, thoughts of seeing my family and friends, having hot showers and enjoying autumn's cooler climate, bring me happiness. At the same time, leaving Atsu, plummets me into insufferable grief.

I am homeward bound. I have one foot in happiness and one foot in grief. I am balancing on the fine line between the two extremes…from this moment forward, my heart carries equal amounts of happiness and grief because these children have changed me, and Ghana has changed me.

I come home with so many stories and I talk about Atsu pretty much non-stop. But unbelievably my mom shares something so wonderful with me. Knowing that I'll be moving out at some point in the near future, leaving only my youngest sibling Cody at home for the next few years, she says they've realized they simply are not ready to be 'empty-nesters' (well, I think my dad would be okay with it, but my mom is one of those moms that can't stop being a mom). She has been considering fostering children. Now that they know about Atsu, they feel that maybe this is a path they should explore.

Now, my mom and dad know the magnitude of commitment that comes with adopting a child. My mom was adopted by a family to replace their infant daughter who died shortly after birth. Her adopted parents had three boys of their own. My mom knows what it feels like to be adopted and she knows how critical the issue of bonding is for an adopted child. They know they will be responsible for making sure Atsu's future will be full of love, happiness and the chance to become anything he dreams of becoming. They have asked me to do more research about the adoption process between Alberta and Ghana, which I am happily doing in my spare time. They also asked me to contact the operating directors of The Last Hope Children's Home and ask them to dig deeper into the family history concerning Atsu's twin. We need them to do everything within their power to find him or find out if an official death certificate was ever issued regarding him. My family is not able to imagine adopting a twin and leaving the other behind.

We've been calling Atsu weekly since I left Ghana, and today the operating directors told me they found Etse, Atsu's twin. He is now living at Last Hope with Atsu. Allegedly, Etse was wandering around the market place alone when they found him. He was reunited with Atsu but he ran away from Last Hope a few days later. It took them a while but they eventually found him living with an old woman in Anagonyigba. He is back at Last

Hope and they say he is settling in well. They put Etse on the phone and my mom and I tried to speak a few words of Ewe to him but he was too shy to say anything. He has no idea who we are and he doesn't know any English. Atsu's English is improving rapidly so maybe Etse will also learn English quickly. What a relief to find out Etse is alive and well. I wonder why there was a rumor he had died... How strange.

We send money regularly to Ghana to support Atsu and Etse so they can go to school and have clothes, shoes, etc. We send donations, gifts, and even a computer and printer. It is one thing to support an anonymous child via an organization working in a foreign country, but it is much more meaningful actually speaking on a phone with a child you know and to also know all the children and directors of the organization you want to support.

Here at home, we just recently had a family meeting. That's how our family does things; we meet and discuss important things together. After everyone was consulted and the situation discussed, all agreed to support the final decision and if it meant welcoming twin boys into the family, we would all support them and help them in the upbringing.

My dad, he plays the devil's advocate part so well; honing in on what real challenges we could face during the process of obtaining a private, international adoption. My mom, of course, raised concerns about how much time and effort needed to be put into bonding with the twins. The most important factor through all this is the wellbeing of Atsu and Etse, and meeting their needs so they will feel loved and know they belong. We have all agreed to help teach the boys English, take them places, support their school activities, get them involved in sports, and teach them what it is to be a true Canadian. Everyone will invest time, effort and love to give them every advantage that we ourselves have had. For Cody, who is still at home, it will give him the chance to become a big brother, which is really exciting for him.

We also discussed the fact that we live in rural Alberta and the twins will be the only African-Canadians in our community and in school. We discussed the importance of raising them with knowledge of their Ghanaian culture too and as far as our extended family goes, we know skin color won't be an issue. We have the kind of family that will welcome them with open arms and hearts. We are all so soft-hearted and fierce-minded when we unite together and in the end, it was a Rondeau Family unanimous decision that our family will soon include two new members.

My mom and I begin our research, and familiarize ourselves with the legal processes involved in an international adoption between Canada and Ghana. The whole family has had police checks done except for my brother, Ryan. He will get his done when he comes home for Christmas as he is away at University.

My mom and dad had several meetings with an Alberta government social worker and she did her job extremely well by being very tough on them. They had to provide in-depth answers to an array of very challenging questions, and she took them through an assortment of hypothetical roadblocks. It was her job to make sure they were in this for the right reasons. She also coached them on signs and symptoms of attachment disorder. This is a very important piece of information – attachment disorder should always be researched and understood completely before going through an adoption. The social worker shared that she has an adopted son who has the disorder and she stressed that it is extremely difficult to raise a child who suffers from it.

This experience has been emotional, exciting, expensive and time consuming for my parents. And has involved at least two trees' worth of paper, so it has also been hard on the environment. It was tough for all of us waiting for a decision but we all rejoice once the adoption is finally approved.

Now comes the downside to this next step in the adoption process. Ghana doesn't have any type of government run adoption process. All adoptions need to be privately obtained and it is entirely up to us to figure out how to do it legally. Ghana is not part of the Hague Convention, and like in many African countries, child trafficking is rampant. The agencies belonging to the Hague Convention must submit statements of fees and expenses prior to any adoption but none of that applies to Ghana. A private adoption in Ghana is not held to the international standards of practice established by the Hague Convention for inter-country adoptions. This means that once the Alberta government approves a couple for inter-country adoption, the remainder of the process is left for the couple to do on their own with no further help, or interference, from the government.

I've found out there are international agencies that market their expertise for inter-country adoption, so after much research we've decided to use Decision Done Right. Another agency we had contacted put us in touch with a couple that successfully obtained a temporary adoption order for a set of Ghanaian siblings. We contacted the couple, Katie and Cam, and my mom and I met with Katie last week. She had a wealth of information to share with us and stressed this whole process could take a long time and can be very difficult. They had paid an agency in Ghana who then furnished them with all the required adoption documents. Katie, Cam and their adopted children then headed to the Accra airport to catch their flight back to Canada. They truly believed their paperwork was legitimate but Canadian Immigration in the airport came down hard on them when they found out that neither Katie nor Cam had lived with their adopted children in Ghana for three months as stipulated by Ghanaian Law. It took a year after that, for them to clear immigration, which caused them added financial and emotional stress. Both of them think the long delay was meant to send a clear message that Ghanaian Law will be upheld to the letter of the law in all matters of private adoption.

My parents have since ditched the agency Decision Done Right. They wanted a lot of money, $30,000.00 actually, and advertised that they could have a private adoption approved in Ghana in two weeks, but by now we are way ahead of them when it comes to knowledge about the Ghanaian Children's Act. When we asked how they could skirt around Ghanaian law and finish a private adoption process in two weeks, they admitted they'd never successfully completed an inter-country adoption with Ghana. Now they hope we will document the process for them so they can learn how to do it. My mom had to bite her tongue from retorting, "Sure and our fee will be $30,000.00!"

After our conversation with Decision Done Right, global media was filled with a story about alleged embezzlement within a large, well-known international adoption agency operating out of Ontario. As a result of the ongoing investigation, reports stated that countless adoption parents were left high and dry in the middle of their adoption processes around the world, with little hope of recovering the exorbitant fees they had already paid. All private adoptions were put in limbo indefinitely. This story just cemented our decision to do this ourselves.

I have also been working with Effia, one of the operating directors of The Last Hope Children's Home, and she is very excited to help us with the things we need to do in Ghana to expedite the adoption process. We will need birth certificates, medical exams, passports and are obliged to meet with someone in the Department of Social Welfare after we land in Accra, Ghana. Effia has already located a house we can rent for a year. Even though my mom only needs to stay for three months, Ghanaian law states that at least one adopting parent has to live in

Ghana for three months with the twins before applying for an adoption order, we know it will take months to obtain permanent resident visas for the twins from the Canadian Immigration office there; the same office that delayed the process a full year for Katie and Cam's adopted children. My mom had just opened new offices in the city so she can't stay longer than the three months. I, however, have been approved for a one year leave of absence from my job, so I will stay in Ghana with the twins while we wait.

It just makes the most sense for my dad to stay home and make money to keep the home fires burning while I go with my mom to Ghana. Also, my mom has trouble with accents, so due to the language barrier and the fact that I know everyone at the Last Hope Children's Home, it just is a good idea that I go back. There's also the fact that there was no way she was going without me. We will just cross our fingers that it won't take a year for the twins' visas to be issued.

During the last week of preparations for leaving Canada and heading to Ghana, my mom receives a phone call from the director of Adoption and Permanency Services for Alberta warning us that inter-country adoptions with Ghana are not being recommended at this time. An investigation is underway about a Ghanaian orphanage involved in child trafficking. The inter-country adoption process between Canada and Ghana is being reviewed for corruption. The person on the phone stated there is no guarantee that our adoption will be approved in Ghana and even if it is, there is no guarantee Canadian Immigration will allow the twins to enter Canada. It is an emotional blow to hear this news, but we are fierce-minded Rondeau's so at this point, stopping the process is not an option. We are willing to continue and take a risk on the final outcome.

On a brighter note, we phone the twins every week. I try to talk with Etse, but he barely knows English and of course, he has no idea who I am. My mom gets on the phone with the twins, but they speak with a thick accent, which makes it quite difficult for her to understand what they are saying. The phone lines are often lousy and our calls are dropped over and over, but we are stubborn about talking with them frequently. Atsu continues to master English and my mom, dad and I have great conversations with him when the phone lines cooperate.

Sometimes I can't even believe this is all happening. I thought at some point my dad would point out how crazy this is and put a stop to it, but instead we are all very excited. My family has always looked for ways to help our community and support global projects that bring positive change to the world. Changing the lives of these two little boys is going to be an incredible journey for all of us.

My mom and I start our trip tomorrow and I'm too excited to sleep. I feel we are as organized as we possibly can be for this bold, mother-daughter adventure. We've wired money to ourselves in Ghana—hopefully it will be enough. We were told by Effia, one of the operating directors of the Last Hope

Children's Home, that four thousand dollars will cover our expenses for the adoption. I'm not sure how she arrived at that figure, because none of the three children's residential care homes in Anagonyigba have gone through an inter-country private adoption process. It's a very big deal for Effia and Selorm. This adoption will elevate their status within the community and in the orphanage business, in a big way.

We have packed four hockey bags full of stuff, as well as our carry-on luggage. We have collected donations of school supplies from Staples™ and have every type of over the counter medicine we can think of to treat injury or illness. We also brought some food staples—all the fixings for macaroni and cheese were high on that list. We play this game in our family – if you were stranded on a deserted island and could only bring one food item, what would it be? My mom always chooses cheese. She is concerned we may not be eating a lot of cheese in Ghana. And she is right—I don't remember eating cheese on my first trip. Well, wish us luck!

Second Trip

June – September 2009

At the airport it seems the bathroom scale we used to weigh the luggage is somehow not as accurate as the airport scales and some of our hockey bags are overweight. They make us unpack pretty much everything and repack them so they all weigh the same. It doesn't matter, we are at the airport early and we are too excited to not do as they ask. We get on the plane, take off and sleep all the way to Frankfurt, Germany. We check the desk twice to confirm our four hockey bags were loaded onto our connecting flight. Frankfurt isn't the most exciting airport in the world, and after wandering around during our five hour layover, no one even bothered to check our passports as we boarded our next flight (so weird!)! The airline assured us once more, that our luggage was along for the ride so we settled in to sleep once again, finally on our way to Accra, Ghana.

On the way to Accra, we unexpectedly touched down in Lagos, Nigeria. I'm sure you are thinking the same thing we were—what the heck was going on? This is where an Alberta woman was recently kidnapped and held captive for an extended period of time. My mom had just heard her speak at a recent Rotary meeting, so we were less than thrilled about this little detour. Carcasses of airplanes lined the runway but an announcement informed us we would not be leaving the airplane. What a relief when we were safely airborne again.

When we disembarked from the plane in Accra, the night was as black and inky as I had remembered from my first trip to Ghana, and the heat and humidity had my mom uttering words that rarely come out of her mouth. She doesn't handle heat very well, but we are on a mission so she did her best to stop colorful expletives from escaping her lips.

We were both exhausted after our long flight. And now is the time my mom gets her first lesson in patience, Ghana style, as we waited and waited for a dilapidated luggage carousel to spew out our four hockey bags. All the other passengers gathered their belongings and left. We continued to wait but finally we had to conclude that our luggage was simply not with us in the Accra airport. We headed to the main desk inside, filled out the necessary paperwork, and were told to return the next day.

I could not wait one more second to see Atsu, so the bags could wait until tomorrow. We went to find the boys. The arrangement was for Effia to bring the twins to the airport and rendezvous with us there. It was a perfect Kodak moment. I entered the roped off area by the front entrance where everyone without a plane ticket must congregate. Atsu noticed me right away. We both ran towards each other and I picked him up in my arms, hugged, and twirled him around. We were so happy to be together again.

Etse was with Effia and Jeremy, and while Atsu and I were reuniting ourselves, my mom went over and introduced herself to them. She picked Etse up. He was quiet but seemed to enjoy her attention. Neither of the twins have ever traveled this far and on this day, they had ridden in a trotro for four hours to get from Anagonyigba to the airport in Accra; a 200 kilometer (124 mile) journey over a typical rough Ghanaian road. The boys have no concept of planes and airports; Atsu just knew that he would meet me here. Effia told us that Atsu had awoken Selorm every hour last night to tell her it was time to go meet us.

Effia led us to a taxi and explained who we were to the driver. He advised us to report our lost luggage directly to the airline office to receive compensation money. The desk clerks had no idea where our luggage was—if it was unloaded in Nigeria I knew we wouldn't see it again, but they put a trace on it and told us to check with them the next day. My mom and I each received a $100.00 US bill as compensation in the meantime.

Our taxi wound its way through dark streets as my mom commented about the lack of street lights. It's interesting to watch her experience many of the same things I did during my first trip and see her differing perceptions. We were then dropped at our hotel. It was dimly lit—maybe to hide the old and worn out décor. The front desk looked like a bank teller's wicket taken off the movie set of a 1950's western movie. At Effia's request, my mom registered for two rooms and slid her money through a small gap in the wicket. The hotel employee issued a paper receipt, which is quite unusual as many Ghanaian businesses deal in cash, and receipts are a rarity. Our room keys were large keys the size of my hand.

Stashed under the steep staircase that led to our rooms, were stacks and stacks of books coated with dust that must have taken a decade to build up on them. We were horrified; books are almost sacred to us. We own enough books to stock a town library and we treasure them all. This mountain of discarded books may have been donated by a well-meaning charitable organization but the inch of dust is a stark reminder that objects considered valuable in one culture do not automatically hold their value in a different culture.

Jeremy and Effia shared one room, and the twins came with us. Our room had one double bed but we were dying from the humidity, and starving so we didn't care. We met up with Jeremy and Effia and all of us headed to Frankie's Restaurant for supper. Frankie's is one of the few places that offers authentic Western food in Accra. It was the first restaurant experience for Atsu and Etse; they had never seen so much food—food that they would not have to divide up and share. They each had a fried chicken leg, fries, salad, and a drink. It took them ages to eat because long after their tummies were full, they slowly tried to eat everything else in front of them. It was impossible for them to do, so we eventually headed back to the hotel.

Both boys were very upset to leave what remained of their food. They didn't cry though; they both pouted by giving us blank stares and refusing to speak. In Ghana, it is extremely uncommon to see children cry; they just shut down and shut out. We did our best to explain to them that from now on, there will always be enough food, but it is ingrained behavior—they have lived their entire lives without enough food, so it will understandably take time for them to believe we will always provide them with more than enough.

My mom is badly in need of a shower—the heat and humidity is killing her. She calls from the bathroom that there is only one tap for cold water. "Where is the hot water tap?" she asks. Oh yeah, I may have forgotten to mention to her that they only have cold water showers in Ghana. I can hear her squeaking through her cold shower. I'll admit, I am also cringing at the prospect of enduring cold-only showers for the next three months. The hotel would not issue two towels for the boys. It was our first introduction to a cultural attitude wherein children are often discounted; unequal human beings to adults. After we are all showered, the four of us all lie in the large bed, listening to the overhead fan that is trying to keep us cool and at the same time keeps the insects off of us, as we each think our thoughts and fall asleep. It has been an incredible day for all of us.

The next morning, the six of us ate breakfast in the small hotel restaurant that only seated twelve people. We sat on cheap white plastic patio chairs around a small table covered with a plastic, patterned table cloth. Our group size must have overwhelmed the almost non-existent staff. We all ordered eggs, which they first had to go and collect from the hens. I'm trying to warn my mom that nothing ever happens at a brisk pace in Ghana, but I think she is seeing just how slow things can move through our experiences. Our tea and juice came after a thirty minute wait and our meal followed forty five minutes later. We are in Africa and we must learn to move at their pace. The bread is very sweet, heavy, and white—my mom hasn't eaten white bread since she left home at sixteen, but she wants to try to eat authentic Ghanaian food while we are here.

The boys happily finished their food this time because the portions were reasonable. Effia left to hire a taxi for our busy day. Effia has to go by herself to negotiate the price of a taxi ride. She explained to us that if the drivers knew they were being hired to transport whites, they would inflate their prices greatly.

Jeremy parted ways with us to head to the university in order to register for the upcoming semester. Our first task was to meet with Mr. Senamu, the Director of Social Welfare in Accra. He was expecting us and we learned from our time with him that Ghanaian Adoptions were now under regional jurisdiction. He explained we had to travel to the city of Ho where the nearest office of a regional director was located. His office had air-conditioning that made the room cold enough to mimic a frosty winter day in Alberta. My clothes had quickly become very damp with sweat within an hour of dressing so I was chilled to the bone by the time we left the office.

Next, we shopped for cell phones. I was absolutely furious to find out how cheap they were. Once again, I came to the realization that Cheech had swindled the volunteer group on my first trip to Ghana. He had lied about how expensive new cell phones were and had insisted all the volunteers should rent cell phones directly from him to save money. Here's to hoping we don't cross paths with him on this trip, as I am sure I will give him one hell of a tongue lashing.

After we bought cell phones, we headed to a bank to exchange our American $100.00 bills into cedis (Ghanaian currency). The bank said one of the bills was counterfeit and wouldn't exchange it, so we were down to a grand total of $100.00 US unless we found a Western Union to withdraw the money we had wired to ourselves from home. I called the airline office and found out they would reimburse us for the counterfeit bill, so we packed the twins back into the taxi and headed for the airport. When we arrived, they gave us a legitimate bill and told us we could now collect our luggage as it had arrived overnight. They gave us a paper notice and instructed us to take it to the luggage office. Once we got to that office, they told us something different; our luggage was in fact on its way and due to arrive—later!

'Later' in Ghanaian time meant we had plenty of time to eat lunch. The most convenient place to eat was right there at the airport. And our lesson: never again eat at the airport restaurant. Only the boys were able to happily stomach the disgusting meal of egg sandwich filling soaked in Thousand Island dressing and served on sugar sweet bread. And it tastes way worse than it sounds, trust me.

After lunch, we waited and waited and waited for our luggage until Effia announced she had finally had enough. She motioned us to follow her to an inconspicuous side door on the far side of the airport. As we stood outside the locked door, Effia made some phone calls. In no time at all, a male airport employee showed up and Effia instructed my mom to hand him GH¢5 cedis. She stayed with the boys while my mom and I went with him. He led us to the luggage arrival area and then disappeared so we just helped ourselves to our four hockey bags and walked unchallenged through airport security back to where the boys and Effia were. I am still floored that a mere GH¢5 cedis ($4 CAD) had the power to do that and equally amazed that Effia could orchestrate it by making a few phone calls.

I had wilted in the heat and humidity hours ago, but we needed calling cards for our cell phones. I like the system here; cell phones are not locked like they are in North America. Companies make both calling cards and cell phone chips. The chips are incredibly cheap, only GH¢1 cedis each and we bought a variety of them so we would not be limited to one brand of calling card. We needed to purchase the more expensive calling cards because we know we will use up lots of minutes over these next few months. These pricier cards prove hard to find, but eventually we were able to buy them from a shady looking character who had set up shop in a side street.

Our last errand was to withdraw the money we had wired ourselves from home. We tried several banks before we found one that actually had someone attending to Western Union claims. It felt like forever had come and gone while they verified our account and counted the money umpteen times. Then, nonchalantly, we were handed a plastic bag stuffed with our GH¢7,000 cedis (equivalent to $4,000 CAD).

My mom was getting very frustrated with how long it had taken us to get through our to-do list, but I told her I was very impressed with what we were actually getting accomplished. From my previous experience I feel that in one day we had just completed the equivalent of two weeks' worth of errands in Ghanaian time. I'm also trying to get my mom to understand that when Ghanaians use the phrase 'tomorrow' it does not mean the day after today. Tomorrow actually means any day in the future. At best, they are telling us it might happen in the next two to three days, but it could take even longer. Not to mention, when Ghanaians use the term overnight delivery, it may take as long as ten days for a package to reach its destination within Ghana. We get to know this very well, as we need my dad to continue to complete forms for the adoption process and my mom has to be couriering items for her business back and forth.

Despite how exhausted we all were, we make the decision to travel back to Anagonyigba so we could sleep in our rental house instead of in another hotel. Jeremy meets us at the trotro station. It is never an easy trip from Accra to Anagonyigba and I warn my mom about this, and truer words were never spoken. The road was extremely bumpy and the twins were overtired so they insisted on staying on our laps for the whole trip. I can't recall a time in my life that was more uncomfortable than traveling in that hot and humid trotro with no legroom, a child on my lap and our four hockey bags stuffed around us. My mom also experienced her first Ghanaian police checkpoint—there are several along the journey. At one stop, all the white people are made to get out of the trotro and line up while the police check our passports. My mom felt intimidated by all this, but I assured her that after a few more road trips she would get used to the whole experience and learn to think nothing of it.

Each time we drove slowly through a village, vendors shoved their wares through the trotro windows, imploring us to buy something. When the twins had to pee, we stopped and they peed beside the trotro. It would have been a waste of time searching out public washrooms for them when that's all they know. Adults urinate in public too and children poop wherever they happen to be. It is very clear that most people here do not understand the connection between infectious diseases and sanitation. My mom is appalled, but I'm trying to ignore her reaction to all these challenges – she will toughen up.

If I thought the road from Accra to Anagonyigba was rough before, it has either become rougher than I remember or my memory is starting to go. That said, there are no adjectives to describe the one kilometer (0.6 mile) drive from the Last Hope Children's Home in Anagonyigba to our new rental house. There are more deep ruts than actual road because rains have washed most of it away. I've never seen anyone attempt to take a vehicle on such a wreck of a road. We even hit a wall at some point—I mean that literally; the van's metal scraped against a cement wall, creating a sound like giant fingernails scratching on a chalk board.

We had stopped briefly at Last Hope to greet the other operational director, Selorm. I knew most of the children who flocked out to greet us and had a short but wonderful reunion with all of them. A couple of the older boys hopped into our trotro for the rest of the ride. It was a good thing we had them along, because our trotro became badly stuck and we would have been stranded if they hadn't been there to help the driver push it free.

I don't think our bones could have endured anymore jarring by the time we finally pulled into the compound where our rental house is located. I was almost giddy with relief to see lights on. Electricity is a good thing; a very good thing! The original house we were supposed to rent suddenly became unavailable, so this house was constructed very quickly, just days before we arrived. The big boys carried our hockey bags in for us. They were very sweet and genuinely happy to offer us assistance. Unfortunately, we can't leave anything on the floor because it is made of cement that hasn't cured yet which means we will have to make do with a damp floor for the time being.

My mom was too tired to offer any comments about our house, but I was very happy to see we have luxuries such as a bathroom with a flush toilet and an indoor shower. The kitchen has a very flimsy tin sink, but it has running water, which is another luxury. There are windows in each room of the house made of horizontal glass strips exactly like the windows of old mobile homes manufactured in the 1960's or earlier. The glass strips are lever controlled and can move from a ninety degree vertical position,. which closes them up, to a one hundred and eighty degree horizontal angle, which lets in maximum air and light.

The main room has two couches, a couple of chairs and a ceiling fan in it. Each of the two bedrooms has a ceiling fan too. The twins' room has a three-tiered bunk bed so we placed all of our belongings on them. Our bedroom has a king sized bed. When we first arrived none of the beds had linen on them so we had to make do for our first night. When everyone else left, the four of us tumbled on top of the king sized bed and fell asleep to the hum of the ceiling fan and the night sounds from our new neighborhood—the jungle! A cacophony of sounds emanated from it; crickets, bull frogs, bleating goats, strange bird calls and even chickens making chicken noises when they should have been sleeping. As noisy as it was, we were all so tired it didn't stop any of us from falling fast asleep.

When we woke up the next morning, one of the children from Last Hope was there to lead us through a labyrinth of trails that eventually took us to Last Hope. Before we left the house, we stashed our bag of money and locked each room's interior door as well as the front door. We weren't sure why this was necessary but we were instructed to do so from a note that had accompanied the house keys.

On the way to Last Hope we had to cross a creek twice; the first bridge was simply a plank of wood and the second bridge was larger, but it had so many boards missing from it, only one person could cross over it at a time. It has a tendency to sway precariously and we don't dare carry anything across it until we've mastered how to keep our balance when we use it.

The walk was beautiful as the path wound its way through lush green vegetation and banana trees. It was especially wonderful for my mom, who has seen all my pictures, but is now here, experiencing it for herself.

Everyone we encountered was so friendly. School children ran up to touch us. They had no concept of personal space. Our white skin fascinated them and they kept touching and rubbing it as they walked along beside us, singing little songs. Smaller children had one of two reactions; they kept their distance but stared in fascination or they became very frightened, apparently believing we were ghosts! We arrived at Last Hope faster by foot than if someone had driven us on the nearly impassable road. There will be many long walks in our future because someone mentioned that Last Hope marks the halfway point to the village market where we will shop.

My mom and I were anxious to travel back to Ho right after breakfast to meet with a government employee who would officiate over our adoption process. The boys were to stay at Last

Hope and attend their nursery school for the day. We needed Effia to accompany us and waited most of the morning for her to appear. Poor mom once again had to adjust to how a day's plan can typically unfold in Ghanaian time. Thankfully, Effia arranged with the priest of a nearby church school to drive us into Ho in the relative comfort of the school's mini bus.

The Catholic priest is a very tall, slim Ghanaian man in his sixties, who dresses in a full length black cassock. I cannot fathom how Father, as he is called, manages to function in this climate wearing something that heavy and long but he exudes energy in his speech and mannerisms despite the heat. The seats of the school mini bus were comfortable and we had lots of leg room, but it was unbearably hot as always. My mom was practically dying; her clothes were damp and stuck to her skin while constant rivulets of sweat trickled down her face. I kept reminding her to drink lots of water to stay hydrated in this challenging climate.

The government offices in Ho occupy a three story, cinderblock complex with exterior staircases. Doors to all the offices on each floor open onto a central outdoor balcony. There is no such thing as booking an appointment. You show up and simply wait your turn. While we waited, Effia informed us we were not properly attired to meet with a government official. Apparently we should have worn shoes instead of flip flops, but she was wearing flip flops as well, so we didn't think much of her advice. It's far too hot to wear close toed shoes.

When it was our turn, we were ushered into an office by a heavy set man who introduced himself as Mr. Senamu. He wore a Hawaiian style beige short sleeve shirt and shook our hands with plump, well-manicured hands. His short cropped black hair was graying and his oval face had enough wrinkles to suggest he could be in his mid-fifties or older. His office contained an old couch and chair, and a filing cabinet with a mountain of papers on top of it that suggested the cabinet was either full or no one wanted to do the filing. A relic of a computer, keyboard, and mouse sat on top of a tiny desk. Mr. Senamu explained that his secretary normally sat there but she was absent today. After he indicated we could sit down, he returned to his old, worn out wooden desk. It too was covered in chaotic piles of papers and file folders.

My mom did her best to understand his heavily accented English but I needed to translate most of what he said. He was patient with this process and asked her many questions. He had a friendly, good natured personality and was very knowledgeable about the adoption process. However, he informed my mom that recent changes in his government department meant that a social worker back in Anagonyigba named Mr. Gameli was now the person who would officiate over our adoption.

Effia began an intense argument with him and even though they were not speaking English, it was clear that Effia did not want to deal with this Mr. Gameli person—whoever he was. Mr. Senamu was not swayed by Effia in the least and said he would be available in the event we encountered any difficulties, but that would be the limit of his involvement. As he courteously showed us to the door, he furnished us with the special forms we needed to begin the adoption process. They were photocopies—not originals as he claimed—but this was the only place we could obtain them so we happily paid for them and left.

Once we descended the stairs to street level, Effia told us we had offended Mr. Senamu by omitting to dash him. Before our meeting, we had asked her about any protocols we needed to follow because we did not want to appear disrespectful to someone who might be very instrumental in approving our adoption application. Why she waited until after the meeting to tell us about dashing him, I have no idea.

How to explain dashing... To dash someone is what we in Canada would call bribing a person. It is an illegal offense to offer a bribe in Ghana—yet dashing is expected and practiced throughout the country. Strangely, dashing is not considered the same as offering someone a bribe. At police checkpoints there are signs that state bribing a police officer is a criminal offense but you must dash them all the same. Each time you buy an item or a service, you must dash. If you don't dash, it is extremely unlikely they will deal with you again in the future. Somehow my mother and I have to obtain everything we need for this adoption without crossing an undefined line between the cultural norm of dashing and illegal bribery. The latter would be the equivalent of attempting to buy a child, so if we dash anyone too much it could completely nullify our adoption efforts.

After our appointment, we walk back to the mini bus and we wait a couple of hours for Father to return. We desperately wanted to have time to buy some bed linens, but when he finally returned he offered to treat us to a meal so we felt obliged to accept his kind invitation. He took us to a Chop Bar, which is the Ghanaian equivalent of a fast food restaurant. A Chop Bar menu typically consists of whatever food the kitchen staff decides to cook that day. The service was fast and we enjoyed a type of freshly made stew and cool, refreshing sodas. The Chop Bar had a humble décor. The walls were made of reused plywood, the building was rickety with no door, and the place had a dirt floor. We sat in plastic patio chairs that had seen better days. The staff brought us dish soap, a bowl of cold water and soft cloths so we could wash and dry our hands before eating. The driver of our small bus was also invited to eat, but he was not permitted to eat at our table. Father also made certain that the driver was provided with a beer. I know what you are thinking—apparently drinking and driving laws are not as strict in Ghana.

It was dark when we returned to Last Hope. Father had needed to make one more stop on the way back to Anagonyigba, which delayed us so greatly that buying bed linen had to wait for another day. Effia started a loud and long argument with the priest when he dropped us off. It ended when he finally gave her some money. We both thought it very odd considering he had just saved us the cost of a trotro ride into Ho and back.

The long day in the heat we weren't yet used to, had worn my mom and me out. We gathered up Atsu and Etse and one of the older boys from Last Hope led us back through the maze of paths to our house. We navigated the pathways by flashlight and each person needed their own because nighttime here seems to just swallow up light. To our delight, just beyond the reach of our flashlight beams, fireflies filled the air with their blue-white light. It was magical to watch them dance their way through the darkness. We've made a mental note to be sure to carry a flashlight whenever we leave the house for any length of time. Without a flashlight, it would be utterly impossible to walk anywhere at night. When we finally got home, we each showered, and once again, the four of us slept together on our bed, hoping the ceiling fan would keep the mosquitoes away. My mom and I were both too tired to try and figure out how to hang up the mosquito netting.

The next day was Market Day and we were told we would be able to shop for the long list of items that we need. Between my mom and me, we successfully navigated our way along the pathways from our rental house back to Last Hope. Landmarks such as a pile of rocks, or discarded car parts, or the shell of an unfinished house guided our way. The paths and trails here consist of brick-red soil that is as fine as talc powder. It coats our feet, footwear, ankles, and shins as we walk. When we arrived at

Last Hope, Jeremy joined my mom and me, to guide us to the market while the boys remained there for the day.

Market Day is held every fourth day; farmers and vendors flood the market square in Anagonyigba and from a distance, they create a colorful 3-D tapestry of produce and wares. There is an intricate social network amongst market vendors and shoppers. Jeremy's job is to take us to specific vendors to shop for what we need. We did not wish to offend anyone by shopping at a vendor who is outside of whatever social network Jeremy belongs to, so we dutifully followed Jeremy's lead all day. We had a long list of necessities to buy; bed linen, kitchenware, a propane stove, a small fridge, clotheslines, garbage cans and many food items.

We stopped by the store that had bedding. It was a wood shed with three walls and a fourth wall, that swung up and outwards to provide an overhead awning over the front of the store. Shopper's stayed outside and indicated what they wanted from all the wares that were displayed on the interior walls and those that overflowed from the front of the store. We bought two sets of sheets for each of the boys. They are made like sleeping bags, except they are stitched up on both sides and don't have a zipper. We also bought two sets of large sheets for our bed. In this heat, we don't need to sleep with any covering, but the fan is on all night and the breeze isn't what we are used to so we do want the coverage that sheets will provide. We brought our own pillows with us, because people don't use them here, so we also arranged to have some pillow slips made.

Next, we bought a TV and DVD player for evening entertainment because it gets dark very early here. Watching shows will also help the boys learn English faster, expose them to cultural differences, and give them an understanding of humor.

Sachets (small plastic bags) of frozen Tampico, a heavenly ice-cold sweet mix of citrus juices were our saving grace in the extreme heat and humidity. The market was noisy and crowded. The ground was covered in trash because there are no garbage cans. My mom could not stand dropping anything on the ground so she handed her empty Tampico sachets to me and I did the dropping for her.

Ghanaian people are very kind and willing to offer their assistance. On my first trip, I had gotten lost walking home on a dark, rainy night and a colorful character, a self-proclaimed Village Chief, noticed me and escorted me back to the volunteer house. On this day, we literally shopped until we dropped. When our many purchases were too much for us to carry, we had lots of help from many kind Ghanaians. By the end of the day, we were back in our little house, surrounded by our new items and ready to set up our new home-away-from-home.

Living in this hot and very humid climate is incredibly challenging. It is winter here, the season of the heaviest rains and most extreme humidity. There is so much moisture in the air, I purposely spilled some water on the kitchen counter, and three days later, it was still there. It won't evaporate because the air is already sodden with moisture.

The moment we begin to move around, we perspire. In no time at all, our clothes become damp with sweat and we can't keep changing into dry clothes throughout the day. We needed luggage space for everything else we brought for our three month stay, so we didn't bring many clothes. It can take up to a week for clothes to dry on a line here so we just have to adapt to wearing sweaty, damp clothes. You would think the cold showers would be refreshing but they aren't.

With all the humidity, mold appears practically overnight. We can't leave anything on the floor or mold will grow under it. We can't even leave our clothes folded. I had a friend who toured the southeast corner of Costa Rica once, which is a true rain forest. She described how owning a clothes dryer was a real status symbol and now I can understand why it would be such a treasured home appliance.

We have now put clotheslines up inside the house. In the twins' bedroom we strung up a line from one window to their top bunk and over to a second window so it makes a "V". All their clothes get draped over it and we leave the ceiling fan on to circulate the air. In our bedroom, we rigged up a similar line. We also ordered a shelf to be made for each bedroom and the kitchen.

I am in charge of the meals and my mom will do the cleaning. Our roles work well for us but they confuse Atsu and Etse. In their culture, family names are provided to members of a family based on what role they perform. Recall that Jeremy is the oldest male at The Last Hope Children's Home and therefore he is called Dada. Traditionally, the oldest woman of the household does the cooking and is called Nana. Atsu speaks English well enough to explain that my mom is Nana, the oldest woman, and she should not be fed because she is not doing the cooking. I am obviously not Nana, so they now call me Momee (similar to the English word Mommy), but it's just a label. For the most part, the boys call us by our given names, but sometimes when explaining a story, they revert to using our role names. We have explained to them that we use similar names in Canada and what their meanings are in our language and culture.

Every day my mom wipes down every surface in the house with a bleach solution to combat the mold. Sweeping all the cement floors in our home is another daily chore. The fine brick-red soil gets tracked into the house. She uses a twig broom that looks like it came out of the prop room of a theater production of Cinderella. It works well enough to gather up an entire dust bin's worth of debris each day. The floors also need to be bleached daily to prevent us from getting hook worms. She sprays the doorways, windows and the bathroom with a mixture of diluted Listerine because it acts as an efficient bug repellant and is much less toxic than products that contain DEET. Our kitchen must be kept spotless too or we will suffer an invasion of sugar ants. They are ten times bigger than any other ant I've seen so my mom is highly motivated to do all the cleaning duties well.

We now have curtains up on all the windows. We bought material at the market and hired a woman to sew them for us.

They give us much needed privacy because children are fascinated by us and think nothing of staring at us through our windows day in and day out. The curtain pieces are uneven and not very well sewn, but they look pretty and we are happy with them. Sometimes the wind blows so strong, the curtains flap upwards to the ceiling. We like the wind though as it offers a small respite from the stifling heat, so we don't care about flapping curtains from time to time.

The first winter rain storms come shortly after we arrive and they give new meaning to the word torrential. First, the humidity becomes more and more suffocating to the point you don't want to lift a finger. There is no build up to the rain though. In a flash, it simply begins to pour and comes down as hard as a waterfall. It shrinks visibility down to a few feet and produces a deafening roar as it bounces off the metal roofs of the buildings in our compound. Everyone must seek shelter because the driving rain is painful when it strikes bare skin.

Flooding happens in minutes. Now I can see for myself why the deep open gutters on the sides of the road are necessary. They work well to disperse the summer rains, but the flash rain storms of winter dump so much more water, the gutters overflow. Roads that don't have gutters get huge crevices sliced through them. The crevices can grow several feet wide and many feet deep. A road quickly becomes just a serious of large gulches—like the road to our house! We have quickly learned to run through the house and close all the windows because everything can be drenched in seconds if the wind blows the rain in through our slatted windows. We must dry most of our clothes inside because the rains come so often it takes days for clothes to dry outside.

My mom cannot stomach going near the market stalls that sell fly-covered fish and meat, nor will she eat any food dishes made with them. She is NOT good with dealing with bugs. She hates, hates, hates them! (In order to get her to come to Ghana, I may have said there weren't any bugs – a few mosquitoes – she is definitely not happy with me in the bug department.) The heavy rains flood the termite mounds so they take wing and create a terrible tempest. She absolutely freaked out the first time clouds of flying termites appeared. They landed everywhere and it horrified her to have to deal with them. Crickets also make it into the house and she pays Etse and Atsu a penny for each one they squish. She adds a bonus if they end the life of a cockroach too and the twins will soon be rich enough to buy their own airplane tickets to Canada!

One day as we were walking along the pathway with the twins, Etse began to scream and gesture in panic. There were millions of marching ants crossing the path just a few feet ahead of us. They were relocating their nest and the boys have been taught to fear them because marching ants have been known to overcome young children and kill them by suffocation. The boys jumped into our arms and we in turn jumped over the marching ants and run further down the path until we felt safe.

My fingers are crossed that we will be spared the experience of marching ants going through our house. I'm not sure my sanity (or my mom's) would survive that sort of thing. I thought the final straw was when we encountered the black jumping spiders the size of tarantulas on steroids. To be perfectly honest, I didn't encounter them on the first trip. But they keep coming into our house and if you even get near them they jump right at you and disappear because they move so fast! The worst for my mom is the mosquitoes. We finally put up mosquito netting around all our beds but the mosquitoes still find us when we are outside. Her bites swell up as big as golf balls and become infected in the high humidity. Luckily, she doesn't get many because they are very painful!

Now that we've had time to settle in I'll do my best to describe the rest of the compound around us. In total, it is close to an acre in size. Our compound is square shaped and the side facing the road is referred to as the front. The side to the right of our house doesn't have a cinderblock wall so two sides of the property have walls and two don't – it doesn't make much sense to build 3 meter (10 foot) high cinderblock walls around only two sides but there you have it. A creek runs along the side with no wall and curves ninety degrees to flow along the back side of the compound too where there is also not a wall. There is just open jungle and pathways on the other side of this creek and anyone can access our compound from either the right side or back side so it seems redundant that the front side and left side consist of a 3 meter (10 foot) tall cinderblock wall and locked gates.

If you can imagine a square divided up into four quadrants, our new little house sits alone and is more or less situated in the back right quadrant – the creek runs by two sides of our house. The front porch faces the direction of the road. Just off our front porch, to the very right, is a large cement well covered with a wooden top. There is vegetation growing on the inner walls of the well and it doesn't look like it is a safe source of water for human consumption. Apparently, a baby goat tried to jump on top of the cover but fell into the well and drowned. We don't know how long ago that happened, but my mom only uses this water to mix with bleach and wash the floors. Along the backside of our house, there is a swath of vegetation and the creek that flows with disgusting brown water. It is probably part of an open sewer system so we stay clear of it. Beyond that, there are outhouses and a place to take outdoor showers. We don't venture over there as it is for the other occupants of the compound.

The left rear quadrant of the compound lies to the left of our house. There is a main pathway running along the left side of our house. It runs down the middle of the compound and is used to access the outhouses and outdoor showers. The rest of the left, rear quadrant contains a goat pen, a chicken pen, an outdoor storage shed and an outdoor kitchen. The outdoor storage shed is filled with tomatoes and vegetables because the people living here are farmers. There is more storage beside the outdoor kitchen and it is used to store cooking supplies and utensils for their outdoor, coal fire pit. There are also outdoor clotheslines that always have clothes on them because, as we've already mentioned, it takes forever to dry clothes in the rainy season.

The front left quadrant of the compound has a large driveway and a house that is rented all year by a Frenchman. The front right quadrant that sits between our house and the road contains a housing complex. Three sides of this complex are made up of side by side small rooms. A bedroom has just enough room for a bed, a shelf, and a small closet. Clothes are always hung up. Drawers are not safe because snakes can nestle in folded clothing. The door of each tiny bedroom opens into a central courtyard. A couple of the rooms are used like we use a living room and there is also one indoor kitchen. Two adult daughters and their children live here with their grandmother.

They live without indoor plumbing and draw water from a well close to one of their rooms. They don't have screen doors, running water, or even mosquito nets over their beds. Though our rental house is almost primitive compared to our home in Alberta, our living conditions here are luxurious compared to theirs, even though the property belongs to the grandmother. Her son built all the structures in the compound and our rent provides her with a modest income. We also pay for our share of electricity and the safe tap water.

Besides the bugs that my mom has a hard time dealing with, water is our greatest challenge. Our tap water comes from a gravity fed water system that runs out from a large water tank located on top of the Frenchman's house. It supplies water for our shower, kitchen sink, and toilet. We know this clean water is trucked in and we use it conservatively. We do our laundry at Last Hope and only take a shower in the morning and at night. The tap water from the water tank is supposed to be safe for us to drink, but we feel better purchasing our drinking and cooking water. My mom draws water from the covered well to wash the floor and disinfect surfaces.

The Frenchman is a cranky person who constantly complains that we are using more than our fair share of the trucked in water. The grandmother and her daughters quickly spoke up in our defense. They put him in his place by saying we have worked much harder to fit in with everyone in the compound. They pointed out that we only shower twice a day whereas he showers many times a day. Last but not least, they reminded him that his lazy wife has never drawn water from the well whereas my mom draws her own well water every day. We are happy to see him, and his wife, leave a couple of days later, so The Water Wars are over for good.

We found out we were originally supposed to sublet that house from the Frenchman. He leases it from the grandmother for about $800.00 CAD a year and then he sublets it out during the times he is not here. For some reason, he changed his mind about subletting it to us. A week before we arrived, John, the grandmother's son, had his construction company chop down some of the jungle and build our house. Building anything that fast in Ghana is unheard of, so everyone in the village knows who my mom and I are because we are the whites who live in the 'very fast built house'.

We don't see the daughters of the grandmother very much or their husbands. They all use a different entrance of the compound to come and go. I think the husbands are farmers because once when we bought tomatoes at the market, we were told it was offensive to them that we had not bought tomatoes from them instead. Of course, now we buy from them and there are no hard feelings because we have shown such an eagerness to learn how to fit in here.

Both daughters have jobs, so the grandmother does all the cooking and cleaning. It is hard to estimate her age. She has grey hair, stooped shoulders and is slow moving. Her skin is wrinkled and hangs loosely on her fine boned, slight body. She is a dear soul who is very friendly. She always asks one of her grandchildren to translate for us when we have a chat. Atsu helps too.

My mom admits she is hopeless at learning new languages so she writes out some Ewe phrases phonetically and keeps this cheat sheet handy. There's always lots of good-natured laughter when the children stand outside our kitchen window and try to teach my mom more Ewe words as she does the dishes.

Our relationships with the grandmother and her family are important to us. We bring her some groceries each time we go to Market Day and she teaches us how to be good tenants. For example, one day she told us we needed to pull all the weeds that spring up through the gravel in front of our house. We didn't know we were supposed to do that. So the twins join us for a weed-a-thon and from that day forward, we've kept our yard neat and tidy. The grandmother insists that one of her grandchildren takes care of our garbage and if their goats get on our porch, the grandmother always comes over and sweeps up their droppings right away.

Shopping at the market is always an adventure. Like the extended family we share the compound with, the Ghanaians we meet on the paths or at the market, are all friendly and eager to help us. Prices at the market have no rhyme or reason. In one store, a used kettle might be GH¢20 cedis ($16 CAD)—in another, a new one could be GH¢20 cedis. There are hundreds of stalls, so price comparisons are impossible. A one and a half litres of bottled water is just GH¢1 cedis ($.80 CAD), however, a case of forty, 500 ml (2 cup) bags of water sells for GH¢1 cedis also, even though you are getting a total of 40 liters (about 10 gallons) of water when you buy it that way. It also tastes much better.

We still don't shop without one of the operating directors or Jeremy along to direct us to specific vendors. They also tell us how much to dash each vendor. As we do our shopping, my mom and I notice that each time we leave a vendor's stall, he or she gives an unknown amount of cash to the operating directors or Jeremy as we leave. It appears as if each vendor is dashing them for bringing us to their stall to shop.

In between shopping and cleaning, my mom tries to run her company via the Internet. Surprisingly, Internet technology here is far ahead of Alberta. We can barely find cell phone reception at home in rural Alberta, but here there are antennas and towers all over the place that provide great Internet service. Her one challenge is that the electricity goes out every Thursday afternoon for four to five hours. Just one more thing we've adapted to while we live here.

Before I forget, I should mention that one day last week Effia brought an elderly man to our door. He didn't speak English but it was clear he was very interested in the boys. As soon as he saw them, the three of them began talking in Ewe, so we quickly asked Atsu who he was. He was their grandfather—OMG! Once we heard who he was, we wanted to ask a million questions, but at the same time, we did not want to overwhelm him. We found out that the boys also have a grandmother and she has all their medical records so he agreed to bring them to us.

Of course, we also asked him about the twins' mother. It caused a subtle change in Effia and the grandfather. The grandfather became uncomfortable and it was obvious Effia was doing more than just translating for us—too many sentences were passing between them. The operating directors of Last Hope have already told us the boys' mother is in a mental institution. Why then, did the grandfather act the way he did and what transpired in Ewe between Effia and him? We explained, through Effia, that we need the mother's consent to adopt the twins. If she is mentally incacpacitated, we need a doctor's note that states that. Eventually Effia simply said to us that he did not know anything about their mother but clearly, there is something amiss.

The boys' grandfather, however, quickly answered our question regarding other siblings in the family. He told us the twins have no siblings—they are the only children. Because he appeared so uncomfortable, we stopped questioning him at that point and the boys chatted with him for a few more minutes. They were engaged but also a little awkward with him. We weren't sure why—maybe it was too confusing to juggle this many changing relationships. Effia used to be in charge of them, now they are in our care. They've had a past with their grandfather, but now they live with two white women who only speak English, they use a flush toilet, and they watch DVD's on a new TV. That is a lot of change for a couple of four year olds to grasp.

The grandfather brought the twins' medical records and birth certificates to Last Hope a couple of days later. We received a phone call that they had arrived but when we walked there to pick them up, the operating directors claimed the package was now lost. How could that happen in such a short period of time we wondered? After pestering them for a couple of days, the package had magically appeared and was at last, in our possession.

Needless to say, we now have some doubts about the operating directors' willingness to help us with the adoption process, yet at the same time, we are completely dependent on them. They translate for us, guide us when we shop, and arrange all our transportation. We can't afford to alienate ourselves from them and feel we have no choice but to keep quiet about our growing sense of distrust.

When my mom and I read through the information the grandfather had provided us with, we discovered the twins were six years old, not four like we had been told. Effia and Selorm just shrugged their shoulders and said it was news to them. Atsu's birth certificate confirms his name is Caleb Lebbih, which I had learned from the hospital when I took him there last summer. We asked Atsu if we should call him Caleb, but for some reason he is quite adamant that we continue to call him Atsu.

We also learned that the twins' father is named Peacedom. We asked them to tell us about him but both of them said they could not remember anything about him except for his name. We asked about their mother and they have no idea where she could be. They did their best though, to answer our questions and confirmed that Atsu was dropped off at the Children's Home by his grandfather. Atsu doesn't know anything beyond the fact that he was told to sit on a chair. When his Grandfather had started to leave, Atsu was told to stay behind so he patiently sat and simply waited for his grandfather to come back for him. Supper time came and one of the girls, Peace, came and got him and fed him. Once he finished eating, he returned to his chair and waited some more for his grandfather. When bedtime came, Peace came for him again and he slept on her floor mat beside her bunk bed. That's how he ended up staying in the girls' dormitory instead of the boys. Every morning Atsu returned to his chair to wait for his grandfather. That's all Atsu could tell us.

We gleaned a little more information from the twins one evening when we asked them to tell us about their past. Their stories shocked us. They told us they come from Kudsdro Village, a mud-hut village a short distance from our compound. The families in our compound have a farm there and the husbands walk there and back every day. Atsu lived with his grandfather and grandmother and Etse lived with an aunt. They loved telling us the story of how they would go to their aunt's to have dinner and then run to their grandmother's to eat dinner again. They made no mention of their mother and we didn't press them for any information about her. We should have—it turns she lives right there in Kudsdro Village as well.

We found out about her in this way. My mom and I had to go into Ho to show the twins' birth certificates to the regional director. Remember, he now presides over our adoption process. When we returned to Last Hope to pick up Atsu and Etse, they were excited to show us they had new underwear. Then they told us their mother had given it to them. What! Was she still here now? The twins didn't know and ran off to play. We looked all over Last Hope for their mother or the operating directors but they were all gone. Finally, I found Precious, the cook and laundry woman. She told us their mother had just left and after we asked Precious to describe her and point out what direction she had taken, we took off after her.

We were looking for a woman in a yellow dress with a baby on her back and thankfully, we spotted her quickly and asked her to return to Last Hope with us. Well, we didn't exactly ask her, we used gestures because she could not speak English and we did not have a translator. We had Precious ask her to return to Last Hope the next day and we provided her with GH¢2 cedis ($1.60 CAD) to pay for her transportation. She would ride back and forth by the only means of transportation available; a dilapidated pickup truck with wooden planks in the back for passengers.

After she left, we immediately rounded up the boys and asked them to tell us about her visit to Last Hope. They were quite nonchalant as they spoke to us. They explained she came to Last Hope, handed them each new underwear and gave a set to Peace as well. They had no answer for us when we asked them to explain why their mother had also given underwear to Peace.

Atsu and Etse's mother returned the next day. To put it mildly, we were dying of curiosity. What was she doing here when she was supposed to be locked away in a mental institution?

She is the same age as I am, but looks older, over worked and worn out. Her big black eyes give off weariness and have dark rings under them. She has typical Ghanaian features; an oval face with perfectly clear skin, a flat wide nose, full mouth, big lips and tight curly hair worn in a bun. Her hands are unusually large for a woman and they are rough looking. She works on a farm all day. She spoke in monotone and her face showed no emotion.

Her name was Awo, and she carried a baby on her back and led a toddling little boy by the hand. The family resemblance between those two small children and Atsu was remarkable. Etse however bore no resemblance to them and we wondered if he perhaps had a different father. (The boys are obviously not identical twins. They are fraternal twins, and therefore two different men could be involved in their conception.)

With both of the operating directors there to translate, we found out the following information. Their mother lives in the same village as the boys' grandfather, grandmother and aunt. The toddler who Awo brought with her has a twin sister so Awo, at age twenty three, is the mother of these five children and has no more. She is now married to her second husband. In Ghanaian culture, when a divorced woman wants to remarry, the second husband permanently bans the first husband's children from the home he shares with his new wife. Etse was sent to live with Awo's sister, his aunt. Atsu was sent to live with her parents and even though Awo's mother had remarried and the grandfather is not a blood relative of the twins, he has always been very good to both of them.

She could tell us very little about their father, Peacedom. He had left years ago, soon after the twins were born. She married her second husband when the boys were very young so that explained why they did not remember anything about their father (or fathers). Strangely, there was no visible connection between Atsu and Etse and their mother. She referred to them each as 'little boy' and showed no emotion when she talked about them or to them.

When we asked Awo why she brought underwear for Peace, the operating directors explained that she could not bring a gift to the boys and ignore Peace because she was also a child from their village. We let Awo know that we need her to come to Accra with us at some point in the future. Awo will need to be interviewed at the Canadian Immigration Office (CIO) to prove she understands she is giving up these two sons for adoption. Her children will also have to have passport photographs taken and we will need her to assist us with paperwork regarding them.

Awo agreed to do this. We asked her if we could come and visit their village to see where the boys grew up, but she told us it would be a very bad idea. She went on to explain that some of the villagers would act very jealous towards her family because whites chose her sons to adopt. People want to be successful, but for some reason they don't want their success to be tied to whites or they can be cursed by their friends and neighbors if they are too successful.

After the conversation was coming to an end, Awo started preparing to leave. By this time, the boys had gone off to play and she did not look for them to say goodbye. We called out to them that their mother was about to leave. They had no interest in her and the lack of interest was mutual. She just walked away. Nothing could have made it more clear to us that, compared to our societal norms, mother-child relationships in Ghana were shaped in very different ways by their culture and customs.

The information that the boys have been raised in separate households for most of their young lives is particularly helpful. We have wondered why they don't act as if they are close. All the twins we have ever met display a strong bond, but we haven't seen that with Atsu and Etse. They play with other children but it seems new to them to play with one another.

Etse is noticeably smaller than Atsu and much finer boned. He learns very, very slowly and he spends most of his play time with girls who are younger. Atsu braves hanging out and playing soccer with the older boys, and isn't afraid to go after something he wants, whereas Etse is very timid. Their mannerisms are as different as their appearance. If we didn't know they were twins, we would not have guessed they were even siblings. Living in separate households for the majority of their life explains why they don't interact like typical twins or even close siblings.

My mom and I have so many questions we dare not ask the operating directors. Kudsdro Village is small and close by. Why did the grandfather tell us the twins had no siblings? Why did he not tell us that their mother lived nearby? Was Effia translating for him or making up her own answers when we had asked him questions.

People from Kudsdro Village, shop on market days in the square at Anagonyigba. How is it that Etse was found wandering alone there, and no one recognized him? His grandfather, his grandmother, and his aunt knew him, and probably everyone else in the small village. How could he go missing for any length of time?

It doesn't make sense that he was a lost, unidentified little boy. Even if his grandparents and aunt abandoned him on purpose, someone at the market would have known where Etse came from. Everybody seems to know everybody here. Surely the operating directors would have asked at a place as close by as Kudsdro Village, if anyone knew anything about a lost little boy. The story the directors have given us about Etse seems to have some holes in it...and Etse is still struggling with his English so we don't know his side of the story yet.

Our relationship with the two operating directors is becoming more complicated with each unexpected encounter. We can't accuse them of lying to us outright or by omission, so we have to take a more circuitous approach. We had another meeting with them. We stressed that during the entire adoption process, we had to produce nothing but truthful disclosures about everything and everyone. We emphasized again that the adoption would not be approved and Canada Immigration would not allow the boys into Canada if they suspected any information was withheld or inaccurate. Effia and Selorm sincerely agreed with us, but our instincts told us to be wary.

Most nights at dinner, we talk with the boys about whatever has happened during the day and about what it will be like for them to live in Canada with us. One particular night, the boys were once again unusually chatty about their past. They started talking about what it was like when they slept together in one bed and what fun it was when they managed to push Peace off the bed.

They are so cute to watch when they get like this. They are delightful as they talk and laugh and giggle through their storytelling. I asked who Peace was and they said it was Peace from Last Hope. I asked them to explain why she had slept with them and they told us it was because she was their sister.

I made the connection right away—their father's name was Peacedom and his firstborn daughter was named Peace. Needless to say, this revelation gave us a huge jolt. The poor girl must think we are horrid people for adopting her brothers and ignoring her completely. We can't imagine how much we have inadvertently hurt her feelings. I instantly called Selorm and told her what we had just learned from the twins. She claimed they could not be right. I told her to get a message to the grandfather so we could meet with him again.

The next day, when he arrived, the operating directors joined us and translated for us. The grandfather confirmed what the twins had said. He explained that when Awo, their mother remarried, Peace was sent to live with one of Awo's friends. The friend could not afford to care for Peace so she was brought to the Last Hope Children's Home last year some time. He confirmed that Etse went to live with his oldest daughter and Atsu came to live with them. When he and his wife could no longer care adequately for Atsu, they brought him to Last Hope, but did not reveal that

Peace was his sister. Then, their daughter—the one who was caring for Etse, got married and she brought Etse to Last Hope.

OMG. You cannot imagine how shocked we were. It was a lot of new information to absorb. No, actually, it wasn't this new information that was hard to digest, it was the fact that the operating directors had lied to us about Etse. He was never wandering lost and abandoned at that market, he was brought to their office by his aunt. My mom and I were both visibly upset and demanded, not in a nice way, if there were any more surprise siblings involved or if the operating directors had any more revelations to share with us.

Now that we know who Peace is, it made sense why Peace had fed Atsu when he first arrived at Last Hope and why he had slept close to her in the girls' dorm at night. We could also conclude that the operating directors must have known they were siblings. The children have strict rules to obey and no young girl would have been allowed to just take a little boy by the hand and lead him to the girls' dorm to sleep there with her every night.

My mom now needs some time to think about adopting Peace as well, so you can imagine how much our thoughts were spinning. All of Peace's records have to be incorporated into our adoption process and we are trying to think what else needs to now get done. With everything that has happened you would think that was enough drama and adventure for one day, but that wasn't the last shock that came our way.

The operating directors then proceeded to tell the grandfather that Peace could no longer live at Last Hope. The poor man started to plead with my mom, saying how sorry he was for not telling us the truth all along. The operating directors' demands didn't make any sense to us. There were many sets of siblings living at Last Hope and the directors had never made it an issue.

My mom and I excused ourselves and left to go talk with Peace. Peace is unable to participate in school, so she has essentially become a house girl at Last Hope. She cleans up after the younger children and helps them at meal time. She is visibly learning disabled so we patiently tried to help her understand we had just found out she was the twins' sister. She is a sweet girl but it was clearly evident her disability impaired her cognitive ability to follow our conversation.

Our hearts were heavy when we left her. She won't pass the medical exams and she won't make it through the adoption courtroom proceedings. She can't state to a judge that she understands what adoption means or testify that she wants to be adopted. Meanwhile, when we rejoined the grandfather, the operating directors had stopped their cruel insistence that Peace could not live there. She can stay at Last Hope and we feel so sorry for the twins' grandfather after what the operating directors have put him through.

That evening, after the twins were tucked into bed, my mom and I mulled over our day. We both thought back to the grandfather's first visit and how many sentences had passed between him and

Effia after we had asked him about the twins' mother and if the boys had any siblings. We concluded, in light of the day's revelations, that he had been coerced by Effia during that conversation.

It is now apparent, beyond a doubt, that Effia and Selorm cannot be trusted. We don't think they want to thwart our adoption but they have reasons for lying to us and we don't have a clue why they have deceived us. We need to watch and question everything more closely. Clearly, they have their own agenda and they are not reliable translators. That puts us in a very difficult position.

This self-service adoption process has become more of a challenge with each passing day. For every step that Effia and Selorm help us with, complications set us back three steps. Every time we have to return to an office a second or third time to get more documents filled out, or more pictures taken, or more affidavits sworn, it costs us more money. My mom is keeping a detailed spreadsheet of our expenditures, but our expenses are amounting to higher than we thought they would be. We know our financial records will be scrutinized and we know we have to account for every cent we spend. Is anyone going to believe these unexpected twists and turns about the twins' family?

Some days it's so frustrating to just work on the steps we need to do for the adoption. We need to focus on other projects and people in order to keep ourselves going. Before we had left on this second trip to Ghana, I had spoken to the Rotary Club of Stony Plain about my first trip to Ghana and that I would be going back. They gave me a cash donation to cover the expenses of building Last Hope a garden. I thought the creation of a garden was a great solution to the constant food shortages the children faced. Not only would it provide them with fresh vegetables, but Effia and Selorm could also sell some of the faster growing vegetables at the market and use the profits to buy other necessary food items. When we first arrived I discussed the project with both Effia and Selorm a number of times. A group of volunteers have recently arrived and it seems everyone has brought seeds with them. We all sat around the volunteer table and put all the different types of seeds we had into the middle. Selorm and Effia gave us wonderful advice about growing this assortment of vegetables in their climate. Then they gave us an area of the property to transform into a garden. It was very hard physical work because there was a tremendous amount of broken glass that needed to be removed from the soil as we dug. Apparently years ago, a pharmacist had disposed of all his glass medicine vials at this spot. We also had to create highly raised beds so that heavy rain would not saturate the plants' roots. The extreme heat and humidity was challenging to work in but we were happy to do it. Thoughts about how these vegetables would improve the children's diet kept us all motivated. The seeds sprouted very quickly and all the vegetables grew incredibly fast. Within a week and a half there were radishes the size of my fist and buckets of fresh, young green beans, baby carrots and beets to pick. I've never seen a garden grow so fast.

My mom and I took the boys on a quick trip to Accra for supplies. When we return three days later the garden at Last Hope had been razed – stripped clean from one end to the other. There was nothing but a few plant stems left. Selorm and Effia told me that their goats had eaten everything in sight before they could feed any of the new vegetables to the children. They asked if we could supply them with a fence around the garden. We assumed fencing materials would be inexpensive but we had to quickly toss that assumption out the window when we found out that Selorm's boyfriend owned the construction company we had to deal with. Remember, Effia and Selorm controlled which people at the market we could buy from and this was the same situation. As predicted, Selorm's boyfriend quoted us almost GH¢400 cedis ($320 CAD) for the fencing materials and although it was an outrageous amount, we chose to continue the project for the sake of the children. Effia and Selorm wouldn't settle for a plain picket fence. It seemed their goats have herculean strength when they sense good eating was within reach. First, they insisted the design of the fence had to be such that the kids could not climb on it. I thought if a kid climbed over a fence and ended up feasting on fresh vegetables it would be a good thing. Then they ended up choosing a solid, panel-style fence. Each panel was divided in half horizontally, by a sturdy strip of wood that resembled the rung of a ladder. When it was finished, the entire structure looked like it was part of a playground climbing apparatus so we all hoped the kids would climb over it and munch away. After we finished building the new fence, we gathered what leftover seeds we had, purchased more and replanted the whole garden. For the second time, everything grew quickly. Soon it was overrun with produce. It was also clearly evident that no one was picking any of the ripe vegetables that were abundant and ready to eat. I finally ask Effia and Selorm why they aren't using this bounty of free food for the children. Their reply was startling—they said they didn't like those kinds of vegetables and insisted they had not wanted us to plant them in the first place. I was so utterly dismayed I wanted to tear my hair out and shriek in frustration. We had had numerous discussions about the creation of the garden and they had been included in the planting of it from the beginning. They had also been very impressed with our large collection of seeds. They bought green beans at the market weekly, yet here they were, refusing to pick their own green beans. They also could have sold any of those fresh veggies at the market for a profit. I tried to change their minds but they seemed to delight in my frustration and I made no headway with them. Sadly, the entire garden was simply abandoned and everything in it went to waste. They didn't even let the goats go inside the fenced garden to feast. It is so emotionally and mentally draining to deal with Effia and Selorm. And once again, I am so frustrated I want to scream! But that will just freak out everyone else in our compound. My mom and I wanted to give everyone at Last Hope a genuine experience of celebrating Canada Day. We bought enough hot dogs, pop and yam fries so every child could have a double portion of food on their plates. Receiving a double portion of food is a huge deal to these kids because they often don't get enough to eat. We also bought enough beer for all the adults to enjoy and we gave everyone little Canadian flags we had brought from home.

The event turned into a big celebration with student dancers, musicians, and staff from a private school coming to Last Hope to join in on the festivities. On July 1st, the compound at Last Hope was swirling with activity and people, and soon the children were called to line up for their much anticipated, double-portion meal. Everyone was going to eat outside on long benches. To our dismay, when the children from Last Hope emerged from the main room where the food was being handed out, all they had on their plates were skimpy, single portions of food. Some of them had only half a hotdog, which, considering that hotdogs are much smaller here to begin with, was not very much food at all. And all the kids had a few yam fries instead of a mountain of them, like we had planned!

Then, the operating directors emerged from the kitchen with platters piled high with hotdogs and yams and pop for all the visiting entertainers and their teachers. The food was liberally handed out because my mom and I had bought a ton of food—for the children of Last Hope—not the visitors.

I cannot find the words to describe how pissed off I was. Effia and Selorm used our food to put on a big, impressive demonstration to the visitors and the scads of villagers watching through the perimeter fencing. They put on a show of Last Hope being a place that enjoys such an abundance of food, they can even afford to feed a multitude of visitors.

You see, they were showing off for the villagers and sure enough, since then, two more families have given custody of their children to the operating directors. Why? People are poor here and they are easily manipulated into believing that their children will have a better life at Last Hope; more food and a chance that a volunteer will meet their child and support them personally, long after the volunteer's term ends. That's why most of the kids at Last Hope are not orphaned or abandoned. Their parents have been manipulated into giving up custody of their children. The operating directors get more children, then they ask for more donations and hijack some of the donations for their personal gain. This business is all about maximizing profits.

The week before, my mom and I had brought bags of fresh oranges to Last Hope in the late afternoon and had handed them out as a surprise snack to all the children. Later, we found out that the children had not been fed supper afterwards because the operating directors decided a single orange each was enough food to replace supper. By not feeding the children supper, the operating directors cut their business expenses down for that day.

So, they did exactly the same thing with all the food my mom and I bought. Our highly anticipated July 1st celebration meal was thwarted and transformed into a business cost saving measure and advertising strategy instead of a rare feast for these children.

Effia and Selorm hijacked our food and used it to advance their business. The children are mere commodities to them!

To witness this firsthand is emotionally gut-wrenching and infuriating. These children are vulnerable and innocent. We had been looking forward to giving them plates piled high with food. To see something we had planned and paid for twisted and used for the betterment of Effia and Selorm's profit margin instead, felt like a punch in the gut.

And, there is more—to add to our dismay, after a long, hot, and very disappointing day, when my mom and I went to help ourselves to the beer we had bought, it was all gone. Yup! Not a drop was left. It was utterly ludicrous. It could not have been offered openly to the guests because this is a Christian region in the country and people don't drink in public—they will only drink in secret. In this case, Effia, Selorm, and Precious must have guzzled it all down or taken it home to enjoy later or to sell for a profit. We'll never know!

It is very upsetting to witness the way in which these two directors run Last Hope. Last Hope is first and foremost a business. It has become crystal clear that the quality of the children's care comes second. I just want to give Effia and Selorm a piece of my mind but we still need Effia's help with the adoption. Grrr!

Well, after the whole Canada Day fiasco, we wanted the twins to start to experience some Canadian food, and I have to confess, as a treat for ourselves, we brought along some packaged foods in those four huge hockey bags we lugged here. We have different flavors of macaroni and cheese, boxes of potato flakes, and some canned goods as well. For the most part, our meals alternate between foods native to Ghana and foods that represent what the boys will eat when we all return home. We can purchase most of our groceries on Market Day, but our selection is limited. We don't eat hotdogs at home because of all the additives, but here we purchase them weekly. They are much smaller in size and we can make two meals out of one package that only costs GH¢2 cedis ($1.60 CAD). I brave the flies and stomach turning smells of the butcher's stall and buy a chicken leg and thigh once a week too. It's not that we can't afford to buy more—the heat simply won't allow our bodies to consume much food at any one meal.

When we first arrived, so much of the food we bought went to waste until the grandmother taught us to buy just enough food to last until the next Market Day.

As a replacement for our morning coffee, we have a cup of hot milo which is essentially watered down cocoa. We came across a box of tea once, so for a while we could really live it up and have one, the other or both every morning. For breakfast, we often have a piece of sugar bread with cheese spread or peanut butter on it. Sometimes we scramble a few, fresh eggs. Etse had been going on and on about 'Indomie' until we finally figured out it is similar to ichiban noodles. So for lunch we add freshly cooked vegetables to 'Indomie' noodles. He is thrilled about this and slurps up his noodles with lightning speed. They both love macaroni and cheese for lunch as well.

Supper usually consists of meat, vegetables and rice which we eat a lot of here. It is a real treat to find potatoes at the market, which I use to make French fries. We brought ketchup along and the twins like it on everything. I also make a lot of authentic Ghanaian food, so the boys eat familiar dishes too. On Market Day, we buy treats like boiled eggs with hot red sauce, yam fries with Shito sauce, or a cob of corn that has been dipped into salty water. It's hard to resist something so salty and good! As my mom has since pointed out, the salty water is gray so it is probably well water. We have been most fortunate not to get sick from it.

We eat our meals in our small living room. My mom and I eat with our plates on our laps—we don't have a kitchen table and we have not come across one to buy at the market. The twins sit on tiny wooden stools and use larger ones as small tables to eat their meals.

We had been sending Atsu and Etse to nursery school at Last Hope, but now that we know they are six years old, they need to catch up to their grade level. Since my trip last summer, Last Hope now teaches Grade One and Grade Two in a new building on the compound. I have emailed a Grade One teacher I know to get some lesson plans, and my mom has done a lot of online research. She wants to help Last Hope with their curriculum and has created lessons plans and teaching samples for each grade and kindergarten. My mom has also created testing processes for the teachers to follow.

The teaching profession here is very laissez-faire. The teachers receive a monthly salary, but they come and go as they please. It is a terrible waste of donated dollars, so my mom has taught the directors and the teachers how to mark time sheets. From now on, the teachers will be getting fair wages for the actual hours they work. But later the teachers disclosed to us that they have not received any money from the directors since the day they were employed. We have inadvertently opened a can of worms.

The directors then contacted some previous volunteers and told them they had a financial emergency and could not buy food for the children. In no time at all, donated funds arrived and the teachers got their back pay. The directors acted with complete indifference to their unethical way of financing the teachers' salaries with donations intended to solve a food shortage emergency. Now I wonder how legitimate the calls were to me when I returned home from my volunteer work here. I donated hundreds of dollars to Last Hope for similar, so called emergencies.

The food really did run out shortly after that, so my mom and I took Effia and some of the older boys and bought some staple food items for the children. After what we had witnessed with the teachers, we were not about to put cash into the directors' hands. We are not supposed to provide any financial assistance to the organization we are adopting the boys from because it could be perceived as buying a child, or in other words child trafficking. It was however, much too hard to watch the children go without food, so we had to do something for them.

Meanwhile, back at our compound, the rude Frenchman's house has a new tenant. His name is Henri. My mom is so funny sometimes. Languages are extremely hard—as in nearly impossible—for her to learn. She's been trying to learn French to no avail, using Rosetta Stone®, so when she saw Henri outside shortly after he had arrived, she runs out of the house to hail him with some sort of French sounding words that sent him into gales of laughter. At least it was a great ice breaker, and in no time at all we've become fast friends. Henri is in his sixties and has white, wavy hair streaked with black that he combs back from his face. He is very slight in build and can't be more than five and a half feet tall. He has a sharp chin and gaunt looking face covered in a wrinkled leathery complexion that suggests he spends a lot of time in the sun. Bushy black eyebrows almost obscure his eyes and give him a dark look that completely belies his sweet natured personality.

Henri has done wonders for my mom and I by including us in the wine and cheese parties he frequently hosts on his patio. He has shown us that you can buy wine in tetra packs and it is super cheap to purchase. He is a generous host and serves platters of crackers and cheese to accompany our glasses of wine. My mom is in heaven, as she hasn't had any real cheese since this journey started.

These social evenings provide a relaxing respite from the challenges we have; flies that crawl all over the food we buy at the markets, ants that crawl all over everything and us, and mosquitoes that are always after our blood. The powdery red dirt we walk in constantly sticks to our damp skin, making us feel itchy and dirty each and every day. Our hands are always dirty because they sweat and pick up dirt. We consistently find ourselves reaching for wet naps to clean them. Here on Henri's patio we don't have to be vigilant about safe food or safe water or safe beverages. And unlike when we leave our compound, we know there is a washroom nearby that we can use without worrying about any serious health issues. Henri has a large circle of friends in Anagonyigba and soon we are a regular addition to his evening socials where we are not the minority with our white skin and where conversations flow easily without need of a translator.

He does, however, live differently than we do. We've 'gone native' by walking everywhere and doing all our own chores. Henri has a rental car and a house girl who does his daily cooking and cleaning. One day he drove us to a friend's property that overlooks Volta Lake. His friend was building a house on a high hilltop that offered an unobstructed view of the lake below. Volta Lake was breathtakingly beautiful from afar but when we drove down to it, the pollution was overwhelming. Plastic oil containers bobbed amongst floating islands of garbage and raw sewage. It was water too dangerous to expose one's skin to but this is where

Ghana's fish supply comes from. We haven't eaten any fish or fish products while we've been here, and after that day, even if it was served in a fancy, five star hotel, nothing could persuade us to eat it.

The next day, Henri's friend stopped by on his motorbike to show us pictures of the chopped up black cobra they killed just moments after we left. Just recently, while my mom was going somewhere by taxi, a large green, very poisonous snake crossed the road in front of them. Then again on another day, when my mom was walking home from Last Hope with a group of boys from our compound they became very excited about something on the ground. They had been walking a little bit ahead of her and they had spotted a long brown snake slithering along the path. My mom brought up her concerns about snakes and not in a quiet, calm way. Apparently I never mentioned snakes—but in my defense I didn't see them on my first trip, and technically I haven't seen one on this trip. She is the one that sees all the snakes! Her greatest concern at the moment is that the exterior doors of our house do not go right to the floor. There is about an inch gap between the bottom of each door and the floor. When my mom asked the boys in our compound if snakes ever come into their houses, the boys told her they do and warned her to check her clothes before wearing them. Apparently, snakes love to sleep in clothing.

Now try to imagine this. Every morning when my mom gets out of bed, the first thing she does is open the curtains to admire the beautiful jungle foliage that grows up to our house. It is such a lovely lush and vibrant green. A couple of days after her conversation with the boys, in the early, pre-dawn hours, there was more than the usual amount of noise coming from outside our house. We've had to adapt to sleeping through lots of noise because it's never quiet here so we didn't bother to investigate until it was time to get up.

As usual, my mom opened the curtains, but gasped in complete shock—the jungle was gone! Yes, every bush and tree had disappeared and all that remained were remnants of tree trunks and grass clumps. My mom waited until the boys from the compound were up and around and quickly went to ask them what had happened to the jungle. They just looked at her and said that snakes come from the jungle and because she was worried about snakes, they cut down the jungle for her. Now there wasn't a jungle so she didn't have to worry anymore about snakes.

My mom was mortified that they destroyed a jungle just to cut down the odds of a snake entering our house. I don't know how many acres of jungle my mom has bought over the years to protect the planet, and now thanks to her, a few acres have just been destroyed. Now, every morning she continues to open the curtains and look out our bedroom window because, thankfully, in this climate the jungle grows back rapidly—almost right before your eyes. Very soon, it will be as thick and lush as it was before she mentioned her snake worries.

We have been very busy trying to accomplish some of the important things needed for the adoption. We have had pictures taken of the twins' four siblings and we've obtained affidavits from all their adult relatives, which state that none of them desire to provide care for Atsu and Etse. Ordering passports for the boys proved to be a major challenge. My mom and I had to travel to Ho to pick up updated versions of their birth certificates and then order their passports. We had to wait in a line up at Children's Services, which was located conveniently close to the Regional Director's office so we easily found our way there. This office distributes birth certificates, so there were many women ahead of us in the line, waiting with newborn little babies tied to their backs. We can look at babies for hours, so the time went by quickly.

Once we picked up the birth certificates, we had to go to the passport office. We walked to that office because it shared the same complex as the Regional Director's office. When we walked into the passport office, a sign indicated a GH¢20 cedis ($16 CAD) charge for passports. Of course there was also the all too familiar sign that said bribery was illegal, as well as another that stated it was illegal to sell young girls. When we ordered the passports, we were told each one would cost GH¢250 cedis ($200 CAD)—not GH¢20 cedis. Outraged, we took our complaint to the Regional Director and ended up trooping back and forth between the two offices time after time.

In the end, the lowest price they were willing to settle for was GH¢200 cedis ($160 CAD) per passport—ten times the normal price. There was no way we were going to pay such a ridiculously inflated price just because we were whites. We finally stopped negotiating with them because we knew we could also go to Accra to obtain passports. The government workers in this office were spitting mad when we decided we had had enough. They even threatened to call every passport office in Ghana to ensure no other office would issue us passports for less than the price of GH¢200 cedis. We decided the wheels of their government turned at glacial speed anyway, so we did not take their threat very seriously.

Obama was scheduled to speak in Accra, so we decided to take the boys there for a three-day stay. We would see Obama, pick up some supplies, obtain passports for the boys, and go to the Canadian High Commission Office to get an estimate on when we could expect to receive visas for the boys.

After a long, sweaty and rough ride we arrived in Accra on Friday, and found out the Canadian High Commission Office did not service the public on that day. We checked into a hotel not knowing that a nightclub, directly below us, would boom out music most of the night. The next morning we were dismayed to find out that Obama's public appearance had been cancelled.

My mom and I decided we'd try our luck sneaking into his 'invitation only' speech—a ridiculous thought considering how conspicuous we were, i.e. two white women with two Ghanaian children in tow. We, however, lucked out when Obama and his entire cavalcade drove by us as we walked along a fairly deserted road. I got some great close-up pictures of him. Later in the day, they drove by us again but this time we were part of a crowd monitored closely by police officers. No one was allowed to take pictures. The police were very strict about it and even threatened to take my camera away.

We had previously met a fellow in Anagonyigba who was very wealthy. He had invited us to stay at his hotel and we decided one sleepless night was enough, so we took him up on his offer. When we checked in, it felt like we had walked into paradise. His hotel was modern, spotless, bug free and had hot water—heavenly, luxurious, and rare. You cannot imagine how wonderful it was to feel truly clean again. Soaps and shampoos don't work very well in ice-cold water, so this place was definitely the deluxe highlight of our stay so far.

Accra is a bustling modern city, and we wanted to expose the boys to some restaurants so we could teach them some manners and etiquette appropriate for dining at their age. Atsu was a delight at mealtime. He seemed to thrive on learning how to become a little gentleman. Trying to teach Etse was a disaster. He became stubborn and sullen. He kept making a scene at each meal. He broke dishes, spit chicken bones onto the floor, and had screaming fits that had everyone else in the restaurant turning their heads in astonishment. A crying, screaming child is something you don't regularly see in Ghana.

His poor behavior continued during our long wait to obtain the twins' passports. Etse's behavior has become very disconcerting to us. The whole appointment was an ordeal I never want to live through again.

On Monday, we finally got to talk with Canadian Immigration here at the Canadian High Commission Office. It was a great disappointment when they informed us they would not move forward with our file until our three month stay was completed. We also found out that the typical wait for visas was five months or longer. They suggested my mom give me Power of Attorney to complete the adoption process after she returns to Canada.

So every day it seems we deal with one challenge after another. One of the most challenging issues we have with Etse is food. Just this morning we asked the boys if they wanted milo (watery hot chocolate) with the porridge I was in the process of making. Atsu said yes but Etse didn't want any milo. When the porridge was ready, we gave them each some and Etse became extremely upset. He knows enough English to communicate fairly well with us, but he would not tell us what was upsetting him so much. After much effort, we finally figured it out. Etse really had wanted milo, but he thought he could only have milo or porridge—not both. When he witnessed Atsu receiving both milo and porridge, it sent him over the edge. No matter how hard we try, Etse can't seem to comprehend that we have abundant food to offer them and that he can have more than one item of food when we ask him what he wants to eat. It is incidents like this that leave us wondering if he has some sort of cognitive disability. Since we arrived here my mom has spent hours patiently trying to teach him the colors, red, blue, and yellow and he cannot master it. He cannot count to five yet and has great difficulty holding a crayon, pencil, or pen in his hand.

I don't think my mom imagined this experience would be such an emotional challenge. She has a lot of trouble spending any amount of time at Last Hope—she finds it so terribly sad. The directors have taken on over forty children, but when they can't attract volunteers to stay there, the level of childcare significantly drops. Volunteers pay to spend a certain amount of time at Last Hope, so without that money coming in, there are even more financial struggles.

We cannot believe the level of money mismanagement that goes on with donated funds. Effia and Selorm will spend an entire day at a salon getting their nails and hair done, and then plead for money because they have run out of food. The children go hungry while they beautify themselves. It's absolutely incredulous. We are here in person to watch how they hijack donated funds for their personal use.

It's very disturbing for both of us to see the way the children are disciplined. They have to stand on tables out in the hot sun without moving a muscle. The caning really bothers my mom. It may be a part of their culture, but it is archaic, unnecessary and makes her want to scream because she feels so powerless here.

There are high-needs children here who require a higher level of care, so most of the other children, including the twins, are used to doing as they please once school is done for the day. It's been a challenge to teach the twins that they need to listen to us while we teach them basic rules and good habits they'll need to follow when they come to Canada. Atsu is a quick learner and has an easy going, loving personality. He is much faster to adjust too. He couldn't wait to leave Last Hope and live with us and he likes to cooperate most of the time.

My mom and I have done more research about attachment disorder, and with Etse, it is a valid concern. There are many stories from parents who have adopted third world children who never successfully bond, no matter how much time passes. Some families write about relentless struggles that have gone on for years and created terrible, chronic stress for everyone concerned. Tragically, some parents even admit they wish they could turn back the hands of time and change their decision to adopt a specific child in the first place.

Some children have been returned to their place of origin in dramatic fashion. There was a tragic story of a boy whose adopted mother put him unaccompanied on a plane back to Moscow. Now we can understand her position and have empathy, whereas before, when we read about it, we thought—how could she do that to a child? We all know there is no quick fix for attachment disorder. All the parents we have contacted by email have given us the same advice; know and watch for symptoms of attachment disorder. Across the board, they all advised us not to ignore or minimize the severity of symptoms if they are present and not to fantasize that love will make them disappear.

Our concern for Etse is growing with each passing day. My mom and I both think Etse has severe attachment disorder. We haven't bonded with him at all at this point. He is moody and unhappy most of the time, so we are very worried. Etse has huge meltdowns almost every day when we ask him to do something. He quickly escalates into sobbing hysteria, but pushes us away if we try to soothe him in any way. He often shuts down completely when we try to teach him anything new. He starts crying or refuses to move and keeps a sullen look on his face for hours at a time if we try to get him to wash his hands before eating or after he uses the toilet. He won't dress himself. He just stands like a statue even though he is very capable of doing it. If he stands like that long enough, Atsu simply dresses him which causes Atsu lots of stress because he knows we want Etse to do it for himself. Poor little Atsu has a big, soft heart and Etse's negative behavior stresses him out as well.

Manipulation is a huge issue with attachment disorder, and even though he is quite young, Etse is proving to be a master at it. He only seeks our attention and affection when it is conditional. Sometimes he will sit in my lap, but only if it means that Atsu won't get any more attention from me. Etse isn't in my lap to connect with me. He stays detached from me but remains focused on the effect it has on Atsu.

Atsu is so easy going, he just moves onto doing something else without putting up a fuss about having to share affection with Etse. When Etse sees that sitting on my lap has no effect on Atsu, he gets off my lap. He has no more use for me. Etse also lies to our neighbors. One of the shop owners began to give the boys bananas each time we'd pass his stand. When we asked Atsu to explain why this was happening, he told us Etse has told all our neighbors that we don't feed him and that is why he cries all the time. This man must believe Etse, which horrifies us.

The directors have not been helping matters either. We have asked them over and over not to feed Etse just before we bring the boys home because then he will refuse to eat dinner with us. They turn a deaf ear to our requests, and feed him whenever he tells them he is hungry. None of the other children get that sort of special treatment. It frustrates the hell out of us when Effia and Selorm blatantly interfere with our efforts. It doesn't make any sense.

When we give both boys something new, Atsu hugs and kisses us and thanks us with genuine affection. Etse doesn't respond at all. When I asked Etse what he thought about being given something new from us, he told us that he should get stuff from us—period. He doesn't connect to it on a feeling level though. He hoards food in his bed or in their bedroom and we have to remove it because it attracts bugs. Each time, we tell him over and over again that he can eat as much food as he wants from the kitchen. He just gives us a blank look.

We have tried very, very hard to understand why he cries, but it's still a mystery. He cries when he has to walk anywhere with us. In the village, he insists on walking in the middle of the street, instead of beside us on the side of the road. We have to go get him and pick him up if a vehicle comes along, but he screams and cries each time this happens.

He cries when he has to wear his little backpack, even though it is very light. He often cries at meal times because he wants treats instead of food. He cries when we ask him to get dressed or when we get him to wash his hands after using the bathroom. At night, he might fall asleep happily but then he wakes up and cries and screams for hours. My mom thought he might be having night terrors, but he is wide awake. If he wants water to drink, we give him some. Then he might decide he wants to switch beds with Atsu but poor Atsu is fast asleep, so Etse cries even more.

Some nights he cries for hours, literally, but shuts us out completely when we try to soothe him. I actually didn't think it was physiologically possible for a child to cry for that long. I thought they would go hoarse, or lose their voice, but Etse carries on for hours and hours. If we try to soothe him, it does not have any affect. Sometimes, our attempts to soothe him make him escalate.

Etse's crying disturbs the other people in our compound so much that one of the mothers brought us a cane and told us we should cane him. She told us Etse has a bad habit that needs to be fixed and caning him will fix it. She said that Ghanaian children rarely cry and she's right. We can count on one hand how many times we've seen a child cry in public. We can't condone caning a child, so we asked Jeremy to come by one evening and just talk with Etse. Jeremy is still a father figure at Last Hope, so he is regarded as a disciplinarian by the children. He did his best to talk with Etse but gave up eventually and basically told us Etse is very stubborn.

It is also nerve-wracking to take him to the market or anywhere there are other people. Atsu happily takes our hand and stays beside us. Etse refuses to take our hand and leaves us, at the drop of a hat, to seek attention from complete strangers. This is another symptom of severe attachment disorder—the constant search for attention with no ability to form an attachment.

I think the hardest part of our situation with Etse is that every day is as bad as the previous one and we can't pretend otherwise. We continue our searching online to see if Etse's frequent, intense crying is symptomatic of some other kind of syndrome or disorder. So far, we haven't found any other matches except severe attachment disorder.

My mom is adopted, and she has lived with attachment disorder all her life. The way she explains it to me is that there is this constant pull and push between the desire to be loved and the terror of being abandoned by those who love her. It's a lifetime of challenges, with demons and inner work that never gets easier. Etse comes from a mud-hut village where there is hardship, but also simplicity. We want to take away the hardship, but we are beginning to believe he might be one of those children who just cannot make the adjustment. Maybe adjusting to our 'white life' is far too complex for him. A part of me thinks he cries so much because dealing with change overwhelms him too much.

It's unimaginably excruciating to witness a child in this much distress because we are here trying to give him so much more in life. It is hardest for us to see him become happy and content whenever he is at Last Hope where his life is harder, but much simpler too. We've stayed and observed him and he is a totally different child. He plays contently, eats anything they give him, and cooperates with his teachers.

My mom has to be very careful that we don't put our needs ahead of his—that we are brave enough to do the unthinkable and leave him in his simple world, that doesn't ask too much of him, if we can't turn this around soon. She spends hours every day making calls back to family, friends and new contacts in order to try and make the best decision here. It is a very painful process as she explores every angle. And she cries a lot because all the information is pointing to a solution she doesn't want to even imagine and never thought she would be in a position to have to make.

It is hard when we can't just take Etse to a professional and have him evaluated, but through discussions and research, it seems that everyone agrees that our observations and conclusions about Etse are right and his symptoms and behaviors are quite severe. My mom, who is ever so hopeful, has come up with one final plan.

Maybe going back and forth from our living environment to Last Hope is too hard of a transition each day. She plans on taking all four of us away on a trip to the north where there will be no influences from the directors, and we can see if he will show any signs of bonding. Also, we will need to hire a school teacher to home school them and help us get them ready for school. They can get in their playtime by playing with the boys who live here in our compound. Just yesterday we purchased a soccer ball and started playing made up games with all the kids in our compound. We also bought these little cloth balls that you soak in water and then use in water fights. We taught the kids how to play hopscotch and other games with the big sticks of chalk we bought. We already have children's books and drawing supplies for inside playtime. On Friday nights, my mom wants to institute a movie night at our place with popcorn and sodas, so that should be fun as well. The boys will still have lots of social activities.

So a final decision is made to take a ten day trip to the northern region and coastal region of Ghana. Along the way, we can interview teachers in Accra and hire one to continue to teach the boys when we get back home. It will take us a couple of weeks to plan everything out and figure out how we are going to find teachers to interview.

We are so looking forward to the vacation as the past couple of weeks have certainly been our most challenging. My mom has been getting home sick—she hasn't ever been away for this long. She has been trying to offset the difficult times by planning fun things to do. Movie Night was a big hit with the other kids in our complex. Now on Friday nights they all come over. We make popcorn, her favorite snack, the old-fashioned way, in a pot on the stove with melted butter (let's call it butter – it's really a type of margarine – you can buy it where you can melt it like for the popcorn or you can buy it where it won't melt – I don't know if it's good for you in either condition) and everyone gets sodas too. The people in our compound are like family to us now, and these evenings are so much fun to host in our small house.

But the bugs are still eating my mom and the jumping spiders still totally freak her out. When she wakes in the morning she just lethargically starts squishing all the bugs that are crawling around her pillow and then reaches up and squeezes her nostrils together to kill the bugs crawling in her nose and then wiggles her pinky fingers in her ears to kill the bugs roaming around in there. The ear bugs are the worst. The first time one ventured into my ear and started their high pitched whining – I jumped up out of bed and started yelling to get it out as I banged on the side of my head. I totally freaked my mom out.

The weather is still humid and the torrential rains come daily. The frogs, goats, chickens, roosters, crickets and other noises still keep us awake at night—I never knew that roosters crow all night long. I thought they were supposed to do that at dawn and then be quiet. People gather at the church nearby to sing, chant, and drum together. That adds to all the noise. This is definitely not a quiet country. There is no such thing as silence or privacy in Africa, which has a way of wearing us down. It was during one of those noisy, humid nights when we were lying in bed discussing the day before we went to sleep that she may have said that if something happened to me she could just go home and then she started to laugh and when I asked if she just threatened to kill me, she just started to laugh harder—it was all so crazy that I started to laugh and pretty soon we were crying we were laughing so hard. The laughing was such a release to all the stress we were both feeling. Yes, we need to start that vacation soon.

The people of Ghana are some of the friendliest in the world. Everyone greets us as we walk about and everyone is willing to help us. Too many offers to help can sometimes be a bit frustrating, especially when we are viewed as utterly helpless. People are surprised that we clean our own house and cook our own meals. Even though it is a 4 kilometer (2.5 mile) round trip to carry our market purchases to our house from the market, people are more than willing to do it. I have even received a few marriage proposals. Unfortunately, one came from the owner of the fabulous hotel with the hot water. He was rather persistent with his repeated attempts to propose to me, so we unfortunately can't stay there anymore.

We've recently met a wonderful couple, Victory and Hubert. They came to one of Henri's patio parties. They have an adorable little baby named Sam; my mom and I fight over who gets to hold him. Victory and Hubert own a liquor store. They kindly invited us to lunch at their place. They live outside of

Anagonyigba and told us to just grab a taxi and tell the driver to take us to the house of the white man who owns the liquor shop. That's all the directions one needs in a village the size of Anagonyigba.

The taxi driver dropped us off outside of their compound. We walked to the gate; a guard took our names and then left to tell Victory and Hubert we had arrived. Hubert came out to greet us and we followed him through their compound to their house. Their place is heavily guarded because the liquor supply for their store is stored here. There are also some factions in the village that believe that because Victory is a Ghanaian woman married to a wealthy white man, she should share their money with the rest of the Ghanaians in the area. The guards are only good if they can resist being bribed, and Victory and Hubert have been robbed numerous times.

We entered the grandest house we have ever been in while in Ghana. They have a big screen TV, stereo, and lots of familiar western world baby paraphernalia. They have laundry and kitchen appliances and even a large freezer. Best of all, they eat western world food. We sat and ate at a real dining room table— the only one we've seen in Ghana. We enjoyed cold Gulder beer, a beef pasta dish and had ice cream and berries for dessert. They are lovely people and they were so pleased that we were so grateful to be treated to such a delicious lunch and wonderful company. Although there were still signs of Ghana—spiders, little lizards and a queue of ants that marched along the dining room baseboards—their food, their company, and their beautiful home far outweighed the bugs and critters.

So my mom has us socializing in circles beyond the people at Last Hope, which is good and bad. Good, because it has been providing us with an escape. But bad, as I think the directors are offended by our actions and aren't being helpful. I'm very frustrated right now because Effia is supposed to be assisting us with our adoption and she has spent more than half of the month in Accra. Every day I call her and ask her when she will be returning, and every day she lies to me and tells me that she is on her way back. I asked Selorm for her help to summon Effia back, but Selorm just shrugs and tells me Effia lies to her too. I feel like tearing my hair out! We are about to leave for our ten day trip to Mole, and we were supposed to have much more done for the adoption before we left. Instead, we have nothing more because we need Effia to translate. We are totally dependent on her because we don't know of anyone else who can step into her role at this point.

I had numerous phone calls with Effia when my parents were at home in Canada contemplating this adoption. We talked regularly for months and she understood how key her role was going to be. Not once, did she waver from her offer to walk this journey with us, yet now, she's been gone for two weeks without a word of explanation to anyone. Honestly, with Jeremy off to university, I have no idea how adequate care can be given to the children at

Last Hope. Selorm is the only one here supervising forty two children while Precious cooks and cleans.

One of the older boys was caught exposing the younger boys to pornography. He had a previous record for stealing money from a shop, so now he's off to prison. That's the sort of thing that can happen when there aren't enough adults here to supervise this many children.

My mom and I have almost been driven off the deep end from watching the way the operating directors frivolously spend money on themselves, while allowing the children to go without food. It's so frustrating to see them spend hours at a salon only to find out that the water has been shut off because the water bill hasn't been paid. Of course, that's when they send emails out to all the previous volunteers claiming they have a dire emergency and a desperate need for donated funds. Again, I wonder how much of the 'emergency money' I sent after I returned home from my volunteering term, went into the pockets of the salon owners.

I don't know if I have mentioned the disgusting bed mattresses the kids have to sleep on in the dorms. The children are locked into their dorm rooms at night, so of course they are forced to wet their beds should they have to go during the night. When I was here in the summer, the mattresses could be hauled outside to dry in the sun. They still stunk of urine, but at least the kids could sleep on dry mattresses. Now that the rainy season is here, the mattresses cannot dry out so many of them are moldy. Some of the kids have to sleep on bare wood now because their mattresses became so disgusting they ended up in the dump. Well this week, a whole load of donated new mattresses arrived—enough for everyone—but I found them locked away in the room Deirdre used to sleep in. When I asked Selorm about them, she just shrugged her shoulders and walked away. How can she let children continue to sleep on bare wood when new mattresses have arrived?

My heart goes out to these kids. They are not being cared for as well as they could be. My mom isn't able to go anywhere near Last Hope. It breaks her heart to see how the children suffer while Effia and Selorm enjoy the good life. It's all very stressful. I have told the directors repeatedly that we only have enough money to complete our adoption and that we have to wait until the adoption is complete before we can assist the children. At the same time, I can't stand to hear that the children have gone two days without food, so I end up buying food for them. Afterwards, I sweat bullets worrying about the money I've shelled out to feed these hungry children because we know how thoroughly Canadian Immigration may scrutinize our expenditures. It is a horribly stressful experience. By feeding hungry children, I could be jeopardizing the twins' entry into Canada. Sometimes I wonder if Effia and Selorm thought that with my mom and me staying here for three months, we would become their own private 'white' ATM bank machines where they could get extra cash easily and often. It's as if they expect every volunteer to be a money tree they can shake and scoop up handfuls of one hundred dollar bills. I wonder now, if the directors have realized that my mom and I have no intention of handing out money to them because it could jeopardize our adoption. Maybe that's why Effia is spending so much time away. Maybe she's angry. It's just a theory. I know I've given in to their constant demands about money shortages a couple of times, but at least I go to the market myself and buy food for them instead of just putting cash into their hands.

OK – we just need to get on with our vacation. That will give us new experiences to focus on. We each can take a backpack. My mom and my backpacks will be filled with all our clothes and essential items. They boys will each take their own small packs for their toys, snacks and water. We take the trotro back to Accra and the first thing on our list of things to do was our interview with a young lady named Charity for the role of nanny/teacher. Selorm's family has known her for years. We loved her from the first moment we met her. She was dressed in bright pink and even wore bright pink decorations woven into her finely plaited hair. Charity is short and slight but she has a big, bright charismatic personality. In no time at all, she had Etse eating his supper calmly, which at this point in our stay, qualified her for miracle worker of the year. As the evening drew to a close, we knew she was the person for the job so we made arrangements to pick her up in Accra on the last day of our holiday.

Early in our trip, we learned that the tour buses, though luxurious to ride in, operate the same way as the trotros; they do not leave the station until every seat is sold. The twins turned out to be great travelers once we were in a moving vehicle. Their little backpacks always had snacks and water in them. They could play on our Leap Frog®, listen to our iPods®, color, or read books. They also slept a lot; the heat makes everyone tired and sleepy.

If anything, rather than see an improvement in Etse's behavior while we were away, his negative behaviors began to escalate. Early in our trip, during a long wait for a trotro, I purchased two bags of peanuts. We were all hungry so we shared the first bag and started in on the second. Etse erupted with a screaming fit that seemed unstoppable. Finally, after many attempts to calm him, we eventually found out through Atsu, that Etse had decided the second bag of peanuts was his and therefore, he did not want to share it with any of us. This declaration of ownership over a bag of peanuts puzzles us to no end. Sharing is an integral part of Ghanaian family culture and one of our family values as well. If only we could understand why Etse thinks the way he does...

We often drew huge crowds of people around us because it was such a strange phenomenon for two white women to have two small Ghanaian boys in their care. Not only that, but bringing children on a vacation is almost unheard of here, which added to our conspicuous presence. Word would travel very quickly whenever we were waiting for a trotro or a bus. In no time at all, a couple of hundred people would converge on us. It was quite disconcerting to tell you the truth. My mom and I were often the only whites in a large sea of Ghanaians. Rarely did anyone speak English.

At one point, when we stopped to get food and use the restrooms, the boys were following along behind us when a woman came up and began yelling at them. She was trying to shoo them away and was quite forceful about it. We finally figured out she thought they were local urchins trying to beg from us. I immediately explained they were our adopted children. The whole episode was quite frightening.

Speaking of restrooms, they are free to use, but toilet paper is not included—it needs to be purchased. Most of the restrooms were disgusting, crude, and extremely gross. Often, they were just holes in the floor we had to squat over. Flush toilets were such a rare, heavenly amenity. Our accommodations varied from small, dark, and dingy to wonderful in every way. In Tamale, in northern Ghana, we ate on a rooftop and stuffed ourselves with the most delicious Chinese food on the planet, while hundreds of bats fluttered just over our heads. Once, we even dined on amazing pizza that I was able to wash down with an ice cold Smirnoff.

We met many kind, helpful Ghanaians. It seemed that when we needed help the most, a kind person would show up and help us through the next part of our journey. For example, a Rastafarian came to our aid in Tamale. If he had not offered us help we would never have made it to Mole National Park. He secured us a taxi by leaping into rush hour traffic to signal for one on our behalf. He showed up with a taxi again at five in the morning when we needed to get from our hotel to the trotro station. Then, he even helped us obtain two seats in a trotro when there were none to be had. He was a gentle soul; an angel who would not accept any of the money we gladly offered him for his help.

The road to Mole National Park, located in the northwestern part of Ghana, was so terrible in places that people walking on the road were moving faster than our trotro. Despite the agony of driving to and from Mole, we have fond memories. Warthogs and monkeys wandered freely around the hotel property. Elephants congregated around a watering hole that we could see from our hotel room. I have incredible close-ups of the resident elephant herd whose members frequent an elephant path just beyond the property boundary of the hotel.

We ate outdoors on long tables, communing with other guests over plates of fabulous ethnic food. We dined so close to Mother Nature, that I had a fight with a baboon who was intent on stealing my yam fries. It screamed ferociously at me as it left with a fairly big handful of them. Baboons can inflict fatal wounds on humans, so I was smart enough to let it be the victor.

At our hotel in Mole, the twins swam in a swimming pool for the first time in their lives. It really stretched their brains to try and comprehend that that much water was just to play in. Even Etse enjoyed himself for quite a while. It really pulled at our heart strings to see him laugh and play with a big smile on his face. If only he felt that carefree and happy more often. It's heartbreaking to watch him go from that state into an inconsolable crying fit in a matter of seconds, which is what happened a little while later.

During our stay in the park, we went on a wonderful walking jungle tour. Wild animals know they are safe in Mole National Park. It was surreal to observe them a small distance away, carrying on with their lives while we humans traipsed through their habitat. Unfortunately, Etse cried so much that other people in the tour group took turns carrying him. On one evening of our stay, while we waited for our supper to arrive, he suddenly jumped up from the outdoor dining table and ran, screaming into the pitch-dark night. Warthogs, baboons and other wild animals freely roamed the hotel property at night, and there was a real danger that he could startle one of them and provoke an attack. Atsu stayed at our table with the other guests while my mom and I both ran after him. It was a terribly frightening ordeal because it took a while to find him.

We returned and finished our meal. On previous evenings, we had visited with the other guests and Etse seemed to enjoy the attention. The twins were both incredibly cute and Etse would happily climb into anyone's lap when it was offered. We had no idea what caused Etse to bolt like that on this particular evening. Etse wouldn't tell Atsu anything that shed some light on the whole episode, so we could not take a chance on him bolting again. We spent that whole evening in our hotel room instead.

The roads we traveled went through many tiny villages. It was very apparent that people in these northern, grass-hut villages live in worse poverty than their counterparts in the Volta Region, where we stay. Between Mole and Kumasi, a city south of it, located in east central Ghana, we befriended a guide named Freedom, who turned out to be a friend of Effia's. What a small world! He also operates a charitable home for orphaned and vulnerable children. Freedom loves techie-toys as he was all decked out with two cell phones, a laptop, a gaming device, a remote Internet device, another smaller laptop and an iPod®.

When we arrived at the trotro station in Kumasi, we were swarmed by a very big crowd that swelled in number until over two hundred people surrounded us! We felt trapped and completely overwhelmed. Thankfully, Freedom spotted us and came to our rescue. He ushered us to a car and introduced its driver as his cousin Princely. They kindly drove us to our hotel. Princely was an angel and spent the entire next day with us. He was a wonderful man; our guide, our protector and our driver. He gave us a tour of the city and took us to incredible markets that were wonderful to wander through. Fresh fruit was everywhere and tasted better than any we've ever had. Princely would not accept any money from us. He was another person that simply helped us, out of the goodness of his heart.

We ended up traveling with the group of whites Freedom was guiding from Kumasi, to Cape Coast in the south. During the entire bus trip, we answered questions and shared information about adoption, because some members of his group wanted to adopt some of the children under Freedom's care. When we arrived in Cape Coast, Freedom invited us to drop by and see his home before driving us to our hotel. He drove a fancy Honda sports car and he was so apparently well off, I wondered about his story that he operated a charity home (orphanage) for children. He certainly couldn't be a hands-on caregiver to the children because he was traveling around Ghana as a tour guide. Before we parted for the evening, we took him up on his offer to drive us to Kakum National Park the next day, so we could do the jungle canopy walk.

In Cape Coast, our stay at One Africa Guest house was a balm for us. It was peaceful, quiet, safe, and fairly clean. The food was very comforting and the grounds were well kept. Instead of conventional rooms, guests stayed in separate round huts with grass roofs. It was so soothing to fall asleep to the sound of ocean waves crashing onto the beach.

We've adjusted to the much slower pace things get done here in Ghana and that is never more true than when one is on a vacation. It took a long time just to get our day started during our trip. A simple breakfast of tea and eggs typically took a couple of hours. Then, obtaining a bucket of heated water to wash up often took an additional hour or two. It was not unusual for three or four hours to pass before all four us were fed, clean, dressed and ready to leave our hotel room.

The boys had never seen the ocean before (actually it is the Gulf of Guinea, but it is easier to try to explain an ocean and not get technical about the labels for different bodies of water), and could have stared for hours and hours at the endless immensity of water. The beach was rugged and the waves crashed with frenzied strength that deemed it far too dangerous to swim here. It suited us fine though, to explore the beach for hours at a time. The fresh cool air off the ocean was a heavenly change from the heavy, hot humid jungle air that surrounds us in Anagonyigba.

Effia appeared out of the blue with Freedom the next morning, and to our dismay, her friend Butsome was with her. She is a slim, curvaceous woman in her mid-twenties with high cheek bones and a plethora of perfect, tiny plaits made longer by hair extensions. Butsome is an exceptionally haughty and rude young woman who had previously popped up at Last Hope on a number of occasions. When she did, she would brazenly help herself to anything she wanted from the supply room, even though the stuff in there had all been donated for the children.

She also had a very annoying way of interfering with the boys during those visits. Whenever we asked the twins to do something, she would quickly come over and ask them to do something else. She spoke Ewe and we had no way of knowing what she was saying to them. They would become very confused; they did not know who to listen to, and no matter how many times we asked Butsome to stop, she would not. At least we could try to take the boys away from Last Hope whenever she showed up but now she was joining us for the whole day—in the small confines of a car!

It was a long drive to Kakum National Park and for over an hour Effia, Butsome and Freedom conversed amongst themselves in a local dialect, Fante. They completely ignored us and finally I asked them to speak in English. The directors always scowled when volunteers left them out of conversations. They considered it rude, so I reminded Effia that it felt rude to us too, in this circumstance. The three of them just laughed at me and carried on.

Their rudeness frustrated me to no end. Then Effia and Butsome began to boss the boys around, and Atsu and Etse became so confused it made my mom and me furious. When we finally got to the park entrance, my mom told Butsome she was not going to pay for her park entrance fee. That greatly offended the three of them but she had had enough of their bad manners and intentional interference with the twins. Freedom decided to forego the canopy walk and Effia and Butsome paid their own way in.

The canopy walk was an amazing structure designed and built by Canadians. The primeval forest is home to three hundred species of birds, unique species of monkeys, and rare, elusive forest elephants. We walked along rope bridges suspended just over 100 feet high. A single plank walkway, surrounded with V-shaped netting was all that separated us from falling from this high height. It was an incredible experience to view the jungle from such a high vantage point.

Etse had another long and loud meltdown, but Effia refused to translate for us. They simply took off ahead of us which in their culture, is an incredibly rude thing to do. They must have been very angry with us.

As we headed back through the crowded parking lot to where Freedom was waiting, Butsome and Effia still avoided us. At one point, Butsome called to Etse and as he dashed over to her, he was almost hit by a car. It was a very close call. He didn't know to check for cars and Butsome's insistent bossiness almost cost him his life.

I finally confronted Effia and Butsome and demanded they stop interfering before someone got hurt. I angrily pointed out that we have full custody of the boys—they are ours and we have had enough! Really, there is no ignoring me when I get mad. Needless to say, the long drive back to One Africa was done in prickly silence.

Just before he dropped us off, Freedom began a long, bitter diatribe about how whites should mind their own business about how orphanages are run. They should just give their money and not ask for accountability of how it is spent. Only Ghanaians understand how to use the money, he insisted. Only we know what is best for the children. Whites should stay out of it. I for one was too stunned and exasperated to debate him. What was the point? He had an expensive car, all the latest high-tech items and lived well. If he had acquired these things with donations intended for the children in his care, of course he would fight against accountability. His statements were so outrageous; all we wanted to do was get out of his car and bid him good riddance.

These business plans that the Children's Homes operators come up with are something else; Effia and Selorm had also shared their plan with us. They wanted to create a shop that would carry all the items volunteers usually needed during a stay in Ghana; including comfort foods and drinks. They wanted to entice volunteers from all over the region to shop at this store instead of anywhere else. And, to win the favor of even more volunteers, they intended to build a swimming pool—for volunteers only, not the children! Effia and Selorm wanted to forge relationships with larger numbers of volunteers, because that put the two of them in reach of a larger number of wallets, so to speak. They also wanted us to fund-raise enough money so they could purchase a car, when we returned to Canada. Everything they did and everything they schemed to do was for the sole, singular purpose of extracting as many dollars as possible from volunteers or visitors for greater personal profit. The children are tokens on a game board, used strategically to win. Winning would mean making Last Hope into the most popular destination for out-of-country volunteers to work at. Remember that volunteers also pay to do a work term at Last Hope. If, and when these two women decide to go ahead and build a pool, I have no doubts, personally speaking, that donated money could potentially be diverted to build it instead of being used to benefit the children—but that's just my personal opinion.

Now, speaking from my own perspective of course, that after our travels and conversation with other people we have encountered along this second trip, it seems to be a prevalent belief amongst the operators of children's homes, that raising funds from within Ghana isn't part of their business practice. Money sources are believed to be beyond the borders of Ghana, in the wallets of whites in the West but there are, for example, over twenty-four Rotary Clubs in Ghana and Ghanaian philanthropy is increasing at a steady annual rate. Right now, beliefs guide actions, and until beliefs change, many children's homes will be run in this same way as Last Hope. I think there has to be some hope of change— these in-country donators must want to have some accountability to where their hard earned money is going.

If you asked me if I think that Effia and Selorm went into this business simply because it was a racketeering enterprise capable of generating greater amounts of money than any other business they could have started, I'd say no. I think they had good intentions when they started. When I first visited Last Hope, they kept the children clean and well groomed. I think the nature of the business caused greed to replace good intentions. During our trip up to the northern region of Ghana, Effia had an opportunity to visit the orphanage that Freedom ran. She also heard the story that these three women told us about a so-called orphanage, that was nothing more than four poles and a roof; they were supposed to check on it to see how the donations from a church had helped the children, but the donations of food and other goods where nowhere to be seen, the only thing they saw were unsupervised, unclean, hungry children that lived under a tin canopy. I think the directors became even greedier when they learned of the much lower level of care some other owners of these children's homes could get away with. And I believe in hindsight, we were catalysts to the children getting even less than they had before.

Let's get back to our vacation. Elmina is a town very near to Cape Coast. Tourists often take taxis back and forth between the two. We met a lovely man named Charles, who prevented a taxi driver from charging us an exorbitant fee. Charles also helped us find a wonderful restaurant at the classy, five star, Elmina Beach Resort. Later, he guided us back to One Africa on foot when we had left it too late to obtain a taxi. He even gave us the name and number of his uncle in case we ever needed help while we were in Accra. He was another exceptional human being—the kind who leaves you with indelible memories of how to be kind and selfless, just like the Rastafarian mentioned earlier.

As we continued our exploration of this area, we found a quaint little restaurant near the Slave Castle in Cape Coast. Tea was served from a gorgeous porcelain tea set and the menu included pancakes. We ordered them and offered the twins a taste, but pancakes didn't appeal to them so my mom and I devoured every last bite as if they were a delicacy. It's moments like this that offer us a short respite from the reality of our stay in Ghana. A spotless clean restaurant with a fresh breeze blowing through it, fine china on the table and comfort food like pancakes offers us an oasis from our sweaty, hot, bug bitten existence. Etse lasted through the whole meal without a meltdown, so my mom and I stayed as long as we could to savor every last moment of the restaurant's decadent ambience.

We traveled back from Cape Coast to Accra on the last day of our holiday, in a lovely air-conditioned trotro. Just knowing that an air-conditioned ride was ahead of us made the usual wait at the trotro station seem easier. We wanted to treat ourselves to one more evening and night in nice accommodations before we returned to Anagonyigba. The Shangri La Hotel didn't disappoint us, but Etse's behavior was as challenging as ever. The boys enjoyed the pool and we all had warm baths—hot water is like finding gold here. When we woke in the morning, we played with the boys, but then, in the blink of an eye, Etse went absolutely berserk. He ran into the middle of our hotel room and stood there screaming and crying. He's been doing this more and more, and we cannot figure out what triggers him. We feel so sorry for him but we can't keep going on like this.

We packed up our things and headed to the meeting spot to pick up Charity to bring her back to Anagonyigba with us. Hiring her meant we could stop depending on Atsu to translate for us when Etse became distressed. Etse always reverts back to speaking in Ewe whenever he is upset. He had stopped speaking any English on the last few days of our holiday, except to tell us he did not like us. He hadn't smiled in days and had pouted for hours on end. We felt so bad that we could not help him deal with his emotions. As we traveled back to Anagonyigba, we asked Charity to talk with Etse and perhaps find out why he was so unhappy.

He told Charity that he does not like us and the only reason he stays with us is because Atsu gets to stay with us. So, it is clear our holiday has not been a success as far as bonding with Etse or improving our relationship with him. It did, however, show us that Atsu continues to display all the signs of being a happy little child, who stayed content no matter where we went or what we did. He enjoyed each new adventure and only became stressed when Etse cried and screamed for long periods of time.

We are now back in Anagonyigba with heavy hearts, as we face the reality that Etse has not bonded and perhaps never will be able to bond with us. My mom has been in contact with some parents of adopted children who have attachment disorder and we are getting excellent information and advice about the reality of the challenges it presents in day-to-day life.

We had hoped that Etse's behavior would improve if we had some time alone with the twins. Our ten-day holiday did not bring any positive changes. We had high hopes that having Charity around would help Etse, in some way, to feel less distressed but it hasn't. We've been calling home a lot and talking with my dad. The information my dad and mom have gleaned first hand from parents, who've adopted children with attachment disorder, is disheartening to say the least. Some children with this disorder never adapt. They become chronically over-stressed, and act out, in more and more serious ways, as they grow older. It's not a happy life for them. After this ordeal I can sure appreciate why Ghanaian Adoption Law requires people to come and live for three months with the child they want to adopt. I think it is the only way to find out if there are bonding issues.

We could not have imagined this scenario coming true right before our eyes. Atsu is adorable and happy. Like I've said in the past, he seems to thrive on adapting, and coasts through change as if he was born to do this. So we decided to do an experiment and let Etse stay at Last Hope where he seems much happier and more relaxed. We talked with Atsu and asked him what he thought and he said that if Etse does not want to live with us he should not have to stay with us. Atsu's only six years old so it is simple—Etse should get to live where he is happy, just like Atsu gets to live where he is happy. End of story!

We've been observing Atsu for any signs that he is distressed about living apart from Etse. In fact, the opposite is true. He no longer has to try to translate for a screaming, crying brother. He can play more with the older kids instead of hanging back with Etse. There is far less stress in our household; it is so much more relaxing for all of us and Atsu is thriving. Atsu does his chores and has his showers now, without making a fuss like before. He loves playing with my mom and I, and he is so hungry to learn.

He is adamant that he hates school at Last Hope and wants to be taught at home. He's very smart and constantly wants to do school work, read, or play games that challenge his brain. He also declared that he would no longer speak his old language, Ewe anymore. Atsu wants to speak English only, which he continues to learn quite quickly, so we are now a monolingual household.

Both Atsu and my mom don't want to go to Last Hope anymore, so I go alone to do what's necessary for the adoption. Etse ignores me when I go over to Last Hope and any time I get to watch him when he doesn't know I'm there, he's a content little boy. I was told that he has not acted out once, cried, or screamed about anything since returning there. He isn't able to grasp schoolwork any higher than kindergarten, so he plays and goes to kindergarten with younger children and seems to enjoy it. It seems to suit him to learn with them because he has great difficulty learning anything else.

It's really tough to think about leaving Etse behind and just adopting Atsu. I'm sure most people will think we are monsters for even contemplating breaking them up, but 'most people' haven't been here day and night with Etse for almost two months. The twins haven't lived the kind of life most people imagine because they were separated by their mother when they were small, and sent to live in separate households, so they haven't been raised as twins. The directors told us that when Etse was brought to Last Hope, he and Atsu didn't play together or seek each other out as we all imagine twins would do. They did not even act like siblings who knew each other because Atsu hung out with older children. Unfortunately, we can't trust anything the directors tell us. The only thing we know for certain is that the twins only began to spend a lot of time together when they came to live with my mom and me.

We've gone back to Last Hope a couple of times to ask Etse if he wants to come live with us and he still says that he does not like us and he does not want to live with us. It is clearly breaking my mom's heart. She knows it sounds juvenile, but she just wants him to want us. We have so much love to give him. When Etse doesn't know we are there at Last Hope watching him, and we see him playing happily with other children; running around in his bare feet, singing and smiling, it takes so much courage to admit that he might very well be one child of Africa that cannot be separated from his Africa. We know that adoption is not a panacea that will fix all hardships for all children here. Etse's distress, and crying and screaming may be the only way he can express a simple truth; he can't survive change itself. Perhaps he can't survive anything beyond that which is familiar.

My mom has been on the phone with my dad numerous times, day and night. When she can't sleep I look over and she is just staring at the ceiling fan for hours. You can almost see her thoughts spinning around and around in sync with the fan. She speaks her thoughts aloud, "If we strip away everything, and look at this issue in the simplest of terms, Etse cries and screams and throws tantrums because we whites are asking him to face the unfamiliar—us! I believe he is rebelling with every fiber of his little body because some part of him knows he can't survive any more change. After all, we whites are the embodiment of change and we're asking this little, very sensitive young boy to immerse himself into the unfamiliar."

"Atsu happily bobs like a little cork in a sea of change. Etse, I think, feels like he is drowning in that same sea. We have the power to pluck him out of his familiar, simple world and plunge him into our fast moving, more complex white world and I believe he's trying to tell us to leave him alone. He has, after all, already been through a lot of change. His mother sent him out of her life and plopped him into his aunt's world. Then, when the directors heard that we would only adopt Atsu if we could adopt his twin too, they plucked him out of his life with his aunt and plopped him into their charity home with forty children he did not know. Then we arrived, plucked him from that familiar environment, and brought him to yet another different home. Maybe he has just had too much change and maybe this is his only way of telling us that enough is enough and he can't endure anymore."

My dad talked with people who adopted a child from Haiti. They said if they could take their child back, and annul the adoption, they would. Their son was never able to fully bond or trust, and raising him has put a tremendous strain on him, themselves, and their entire family.

Another thought we wrestle with concerns keeping these twins together no matter what. Atsu wants to live with us. If we leave Atsu here and deny him a life with us just because he is a twin, that would feel like punishment to him. Why should Atsu be punished just because his twin can't bond? Why should Atsu be denied a life he clearly loves, just because two eggs became fertilized at the same time instead of one? Living with a white family in an all-white rural community, in a place where it snows and gets really cold, is the epitome of change. Atsu shows that he thrives on change. Etse shows that change is his worst nightmare. This whole chapter of our lives may not have a happy ending. Waiting for my parents to make their decision seems like forever, but it will forever change lives no matter what is decided.

Talking about change! There have been some really pleasant changes to our household now that Charity is living with us. She insists on beginning her day at 4 a.m. so she has time to do laundry and clean our house. In fact, she has even taken over the cooking and shopping. Charity explained to us that it is her responsibility to take care of us in this way. Now that she lives with us, if we do any chores, the people in the village will think Charity is not taking care of us well enough and that will ruin her reputation.

One evening, my mom mentioned that the usual evening singing, that took place at the church close by had stopped. Charity told us that they had not been singing songs—they had been chanting curses at us because we had not hired a Ghanaian house girl to do our cooking, cleaning and shopping. Villagers, although polite and helpful, actually considered us greedy and selfish because they perceive that white people have lots of money, but we would not part with a little bit of it to hire someone. It is so interesting that within our compound, our efforts to fit in and do things for ourselves has created positive relationships with the other people living in the compound, but caused resentment amongst the villagers.

Charity does not understand why we are not bothered or scared about curses and voodoo. She, like many Ghanaians, believes in it completely. Charity's legs are covered in large black blotches. When Ghanaians injure their skin, the scarring is dark black. She got her scars after she contracted some sort of fungal infection in her youth. She sought the help of witch doctors, and the infection spread, and by the looks of her scars, it got quite bad.

My mom and I have been teaching Charity how to teach Atsu at home. She's also learning how to create menus, plan meals and combine foods for better nutrition. We've shared what our budget is for Market Days because, as I said before, she also does the shopping now.

We learned something interesting about house girls from our friend Victory. She has a house girl, as do most middle and upper class Ghanaian households. The girl's mother gave her to Victory and in exchange, Victory was to provide the girl with an education. Ghanaians don't refer to their house girls or house boys as slaves, but essentially, that is what they are. Victory's house girl did not want to go to school and in Ghana, attendance at schools is not mandatory. She did not perform her chores very well in Victory and Hubert's household so Victory returned her to her mother. This is turn, brought disgrace to her mother. Without an education, there are very few opportunities for Ghanaian children beyond slavery or prostitution.

Charity is not our house girl, we pay her to be Atsu's school teacher. But because she lives with us she has to do all the work the same as a house girl or her reputation amongst her people will be in ruins.

One night, when my mom and I were passing by Last Hope on our way home from Anagonyigba, one of the girls came out to tell us that a young girl named Sarah was very sick. We followed the girl into the building and asked where Effia, Selorm, and Precious were. They had left and no one knew where they'd gone. The older kids were off somewhere and the younger kids were just hanging around watching TV. We went into the girl's dorm and Sarah was lying there burning up with fever. We tried calling Effia and Selorm but neither of them answered their cell phones. My mom and I decided to take Sarah home.

When we arrived at our house with Sarah, her temperature was 41 degrees Celsius (106 degrees Fahrenheit). We gave her some children's acetaminophen and sponged her body with tepid water to cool her off. Charity became very concerned. She said that Effia and Selorm were going to be very angry with us for taking Sarah. Within a half hour, we got Sarah's fever down to 38.8

degrees Celsius (102 degrees Fahrenheit). Sure enough, Selorm finally called me back and she was livid. She demanded that we return Sarah to Last Hope immediately. Selorm was very concerned that someone may have seen us take Sarah and therefore, could potentially start a rumor that they, the directors, were not caring for the children well enough at Last Hope. Even when a child was seriously ill, Selorm and Effia put the welfare of their business ahead of that of the child's.

Charity and I only took Sarah back to Last Hope after we were sure her fever was staying down. We really thought she would have died had we not intervened when we did. The next morning, Charity and I got up at 5 a.m. and returned to Last Hope to pick Sarah up and take her to the hospital. The directors, however, wouldn't let us just take Sarah. In return for allowing us to take Sarah, we had to take four other children with us to the hospital. Two of them were new arrivals that had ringworm and were to be tested for HIV. The two others had malaria, which was what poor Sarah was infected with. Of course, none of the children had medical cards, so I was to pay to acquire them and then pay for the children's treatment as well. Thankfully, all three children with malaria recovered, but Sarah is an example of how gravely ill people can become when they contract malaria.

After weeks of trying to bond with Etse to no avail, my parents have decided they cannot adopt him. This decision has come after weeks of emotional turmoil. He has not bonded with us despite our best efforts, and in fact, acts quite traumatized when he is forced to socialize with us. Part of the adoption process here requires a child of their age to stand before a judge and answer questions about whether or not they want to be adopted by the people requesting the court to grant an adoption. Since Etse has gone back to live at Last Hope, we have asked him a number of times if he wants to come back and live with us. His answer is always the same. He doesn't like us! If he is asked by a judge if he wants us to adopt him, there is zero chance that his answer will be any different. Remember that Etse has an older sister who also lives at Last Hope, so he is very content when he is there.

Needless to say, we are all very upset by this unexpected outcome. My parents have done a lot of soul searching before arriving at this decision. We, as a family, are united in our firm belief that Atsu should not be denied a life with us—one that he wants very much—just because his twin suffers from attachment disorder.

So, after the excruciating decision to adopt only Atsu was made, we had to return to the regional director's office in Ho to apprise him of the change. Mr. Senamu was quite disinterested in our news, but informed us that judges took their vacations in August and September so adoption hearings could not be booked until October. We explained to him that my mom had to return to Canada in September and that we needed a court date before then. He then told us there were travelling judges that filled in for their vacationing peers and that he would try to get a court date with one of them.

After paying him his customary dash, we left. A few days later, he called and much to our relief, he had booked a hearing for us on August 25. We explained to him that this date was a few days shy of our obligatory three month stay in Ghana, but he assured us all would be well. This was the only date and time available. The alternative was to wait until October, so needless to say we jumped into high gear. Effia had slowed us down incredibly with her multiple disappearing acts from Anagonyigba, and we still had to file many court documents. However, a court assistant was then assigned to our case, so we no longer had to travel the horrible roads to Ho and back. He took all the necessary documents back and forth between Ho and Anagonyigba and filed them in court on our behalf.

We registered all the passport pictures of Atsu's siblings with the court. Then, we arranged transportation for Atsu's Aunt and Uncle, his mother, and his grandfather to meet us at the court house so we could obtain affidavits from them, stating they had no intention to care for Atsu. All his relatives were happy to see him and excited about his adoption. Atsu's grandfather had never learned to read or write so he signed the paperwork with his thumbprint as his signature.

When we completed everything, the court officer requested his dash. My mom gave him about GH¢20 cedis ($16 CAD). He was very upset and demanded ten times that amount but she refused to pay it. She asked Effia to tell him that she was quite happy to pay a reasonable amount for his services, but that she would absolutely not, under any circumstances, pay the huge amount he had demanded because it would constitute bribery. She would not do anything to risk our adoption. Her stern voice put an end to his outrageous request in record time. Some things don't require translation. Tone can say it all. Go mom!

I lost count of the number of times my mom and I pored over our pile of documents again and again, checking, double-checking, and triple-checking that we had everything we needed in our file. We had compiled our adoption application independently; figuring out a way around countless obstacles and frustrations that came with doing business in Ghana. We had scaled a very slippery slope the entire time, dashing people adequately, but refusing to pay bribes to anyone.

We bought Atsu a new shirt made from fabric that had a tribal print pattern. Then we bought him new pants and sandals. The day before our court date, my mom and I returned to Last Hope to ask Etse one last time if he wanted to come and live with us. His answer was no different—he did not like us and wanted to stay at Last Hope. It is incredibly sad to think of the future that might have been Etse's, but his attitude is understandable. He has been rejected by his mother, and neglected for much of his young life. He has demonstrated that he is unable to bond to us or adapt to the changes that living with whites would require of him. Even though my head understands this, my heart aches having to leave him behind. Everyone in our family has an aching heart for Etse and a happy heart for Atsu.

Later that day, I asked Atsu for his thoughts. He told us he was very excited to be adopted because he loved us and liked living with us. After that, he added that he was also excited because his skin would turn peach and he would talk perfect English the moment his adoption was completed. What a shocker that was! We don't know where he got that idea from but we could hardly keep a straight face as we explained the truth to him—his skin would stay the same and he would still need to work on his English. No matter—he still had a big smile on his face and his dark brown eyes still twinkled with happiness.

The big day arrived and Atsu, Charity, Effia, my mom and I went by taxi to Ho. When we arrived at the courthouse, the old, colonial style building housed an atmosphere of quiet respect. It had no windows, just wooden shutters that opened to allow air to flow through the courtroom. The judge called us into his chambers and the regional director, Mr. Senamu, introduced us. The judge briefly went through our documents and then started to talk with Atsu. He asked Atsu if he liked his new family and if he wanted to be adopted and move to Canada. Atsu was shy but he answered confidently, and added that he was happy and loved us. He was completely genuine and there was no mistaking the sincerity of his words.

Then the judge directed his questions to my mom. He wanted to know if she would return in two years to finalize the adoption. I interrupted and said that it would be very expensive to come back again all the way from Canada. My mom quickly added that we would do whatever was asked of us to finalize this adoption. She didn't want to give the judge the impression that we wanted any type of favoritism from the court.

I think he liked us and respected the fact that we had compiled all our legal documents on our own. He then went on to say that he had the authority to either grant a temporary adoption that would require us to return in two years to complete it, or provide us with a permanent adoption at this hearing. He mentioned the long trip we had undergone from Canada to Ghana and commended us for living in Ghana for the last three months. He talked about the best possible decisions we had made for each of the boys and when he acknowledged our decision to leave Etse where he felt safe and content, it touched both my mom and I in an incredible way. Then, just like that, he granted us a permanent adoption. He told Caleb—for that name, not Atsu, was on all the documents—that he was a very lucky boy and urged him to remember his day of adoption for the rest of his life. In closing, he pointed out that Caleb would be living in better conditions than he, a judge, lived here in Ghana.

We could not have been more stunned by his words! We had never entertained the possibility that a permanent adoption might be granted while we were here. It was amazing news because it meant that Caleb could now become a Canadian Citizen, rather than a landed immigrant. After the judge dismissed us, we thanked Mr. Senamu and then headed for a restaurant to celebrate. The first time I referred to Atsu as Atsu, he firmly announced that because he was now adopted and the judge had said his name was Caleb, he was no longer Atsu. In his mind, the adoption was transformative and this was his way of dealing with it. The directors at Last Hope had given him the name Atsu but his family had always called him Caleb. Now he wanted his new family to call him Caleb and never call him Atsu again.

We taxied back to Last Hope to drop Effia off. Caleb was standing tall and proud. Everyone could see he no longer considered himself one of them. His body language spoke volumes, 'I am beyond your reach now.' Selorm became furious when she saw Caleb's new confidence. She pointed at him and in a vile tone, declared she would always maintain more control over him than we would ever have and that no matter how many years Caleb lived in Canada, the moment she called him Atsu, he would always do her bidding. We took our leave abruptly and as we walked home, we explained to Caleb that he would never, ever have to do anything that Effia and Selorm told him to do and that we would always protect him from them.

After we arrived at our house I decided in a moment of insanity to spill frozen yogurt all over my mom. Then, because I was laughing hysterically, I could hardly get out the words, "I'm sorry." Caleb stepped in and told us quite adamantly that because her skin is peach and my skin is peach, we don't have to say sorry to each other. Only people that have skin a different color than peach have to say sorry to peach-skinned people. I can't even make this stuff up! He is too funny.

Now that we have completed Caleb's adoption, we must begin the process of obtaining a visa for him from the Canadian Immigration Department in Accra. He cannot board a plane bound for Canada until he has one. We all keep our fingers crossed that it will happen sooner, rather than later.

My mom was keeping up a brave face throughout the process. We are very bonded. We tell each other everything. But when I came across this letter, it made me realize there was so much more going on for her during these last days in Ghana.

Dearest Bonnie,

Oh my God! I just wrote and sent off an email update to everyone about our permanent adoption hearing. It is a true time of celebration. But there is so much more going on. Mandi, Caleb, and Charity are fast asleep but I'm too heartbroken to sleep. You, more than anyone else, know and understand how painful it is for me to live with our decision not to adopt Etse. My head knows we have made the best decision for him but my heart is a mess.

You know from our talks about the lifelong struggles I've had fighting the effects of being abandoned by my birth mother. It is almost impossible for me to trust that someone who comes into my life and states they love me will stay. I still need constant reassurance that I am loved by my loved ones, because I continually battle the voice inside my head that insists they might unexpectedly leave me one day. You know how hard I've worked to heal enough so I can let people in, trust them, and risk loving them back.

It has taken me decades of effort to get this far. There is no cure for attachment disorder—for some lucky ones, like me, you learn enough skills to live with it—to live alongside what it does to your insides for the rest of your life! I still remember every single person who I pushed away in my past, when they tried to offer me love. I knew that what I was doing hurt them deeply, but because I could not risk, I just shut down completely!

It's so hard for other people to understand that I did not feel sad or sorry. I felt no guilt or regret after I pushed them away for good. I would go to a state that was devoid of emotion. It was nothingness, and feelings do not exist there.

When my heart gets involved—when I give love—it is such a messy business. Love is the greatest feeling in the world but for people like me, there is always a price to pay. There is a dark side to the joy and happiness. Uncontrollable thoughts and feelings run rampant each time I open my heart to someone. Imaginary scenarios bully their way through my thoughts; who will leave first, how will they trash my trust, are there any clues that they are planning to deceive me?

You know that it took most of my life to unlearn the testing game I put everyone who loved me through. When one of them would profess love, I would push them away over and over again to find out if they would come back or just leave. As I learned to trust and love people, it became a push and pull game. Part of me would push them away because I feared they'd leave me anyway, and then the part of me that loved them would pull them back in. I can only let a few people into my circle of love because it takes so much work to deal with my messed up heart.

I love Etse. It is that plain and simple. I love him with every fiber of my being, just as I love Caleb, my newly adopted son. He is seeking but he is so shut down he cannot see what he is searching for. I recognize his search. He is seeking a feeling place, an emotional mix of love, trust and security. He cannot find it because he is full of nothingness, more so than I ever was. Tragically, he can't even relate to those emotions anymore.

I know his state of nothingness. He is in extreme survivor mode and his nothingness is his only security. I see it in his eyes and I see it when he freezes his features. I know from my own experience and from everything I've studied, that once you shut down to that degree it is almost impossible to reconnect again.

I'm white and I live in Canada, in a familiar society and culture. It feels like I've had to crawl over miles of broken glass, drag myself along by my fingernails, and tread dangerous waters for years to get to where I am today. Could I have come this far if some strangers had taken me away from all that was familiar to me when I was just six? Could I have learned to bond with loved ones if I'd been taken to a foreign land with a foreign culture, where no one spoke my mother tongue? I honestly believe the answer is no!

At the same time Bonnie, I want to bring Etse home so badly because I don't want to be another person that abandons him. But as soon as I admit that thought, I realize this whole experience with Etse is triggering my own memories of abandonment. My heart is breaking because I don't want to do to Etse what my birth mother did to me.

When I am able to walk successfully across the hot, fiery coals of my abandonment issues and give my love to someone, fierceness grows in my heart. I become a warrior and nothing a loved one does will ever compromise my love for them. Maybe it's because I have to win an almost impossible battle just to be able to love. When I give love, it is intense and now, Bonnie, my head is asking my heart to walk away from Etse whom I love and it is tearing me apart.

The night we took him back to Last Hope with all his things, the deep black evening hid my tears from everyone. That was when the nightmares started. They are so real, spilling over with immense emotions. Fear pierces me like bullets, leaving holes for my vulnerability to leak out. I dream that Etse is crying for me but I can't find him. What if I don't find him in time? I search, running through a never-ending maze of paths and streets while his cries fade away. In and out, through the twists and turns I go—I can't stop even though I no longer hear him.

Then, I am lost in the nothingness. Panic entombs me. My heart beats a wild rhythm of fear mixed with the devastation of losing a loved one. It doesn't break though. It swells more and more with each beat until it squeezes my lungs so hard, I cannot take a proper breath in or out. My blood disappears into the ether and I turn cold. My eyes see but everything is nothingness. My brain freezes. My palms get clammy and my skin hurts. It feels like it is being peeled off of me, inch by inch. I am so raw I want to wail and scream out my pain but my throat hurts like when I had my tonsils taken out. When I wake up, my every cell needs me to cry for him but I don't because I still have to strain my ears to hear a sound that no longer exists. I am listening for Etse's cries and then my heart breaks anew when I remember that Etse no longer cries—he is happy now because he is back where he belongs— away from us whites.

I don't see Etse anymore, Bonnie. We avoid going to Last Hope as much as possible. When we do need to go there, Mandi sees him but I don't. My eyes might look at him but my brain won't allow me to process that he is there, right in front of me. Later Mandi will say something about Etse doing this or that, and I'm sure she thinks I am crazy or blind because I say I did not see him.

That's my truth. I cannot allow myself to see him because if I do that—look at him—my grief will slam me like a fatal blow. I am doing what I need to do to survive our difficult decision about Etse because I know it is the best thing for him. I knew it would take courage to face the darkness that still lives in me.

You've been with me when I've lost loved ones before, Bonnie. It's hard when loved ones die but this is so much harder. I can feel Etse like there is a special wire that runs from his heart into mine that vibrates with each beat of our bonded hearts. I'm not being melodramatic. Etse will be physically gone from my life when we return to Canada but I will carry him in my heart until the day I die.

I know I can do this Bonnie. I just had to share my insides with someone. My mother-heart is indomitable and I have a happy, content, delightful six year old son with dark skin, round black, twinkling eyes and an unconquerable spirit who can hardly wait to begin his life in Canada. OK my dear, dear friend. I miss you terribly and can hardly wait to introduce you to our adorable new son!

Lots of love...Kat

It's nearing the end of August now, and we still have work to do before my mom goes home. She's been trying to call my dad because she had a very frustrating call this afternoon. She called the Director of Children's Services back home. This Director is the one who told us it was unlikely we'd get an adoption done in Ghana at this time because the Canadian government was in the midst of an investigation about alleged child trafficking in some of the orphanages in Ghana. My mom called her to secure a copy of the Letter of No Involvement that we need for Caleb's visa application.

The Director told my mom with intense vehemence, that in her professional opinion it was absolutely wrong to split up the twins.

My mom tried to explain all the factors that were involved in our difficult decision, but she just kept talking over her. The Director also told her, in no uncertain terms, that if she had the power, she would stop our adoption and not allow Caleb to leave Ghana. Then, as if that wasn't enough, the Director went on to tell her she was going to phone all her contacts to see if there is a legal loophole somewhere that would give someone in the Canadian government the power to deny our adoption of just one twin.

Will this endless roller coaster ride ever end? I feel like my mom and I are all doing the equivalent of an emotional, energy draining Ironman Triathlon in Ghana, that doesn't have a finish line. My mom and I have sky high anxiety that our phone is going to ring at any minute telling us Caleb will never be ours. My mom is not sleeping, so at night she combs through legal stuff on the Internet, trying to find information on whether or not our government has the right, at this stage, to annul our adoption because we are splitting up the twins. I think if there was such a law, she would have found it by now. It can't be that obscure, can it? Anyway, I know the woman my mom spoke with had no choice but to do her job and send us the Letter of No Involvement despite her personal or professional objections. We've already received an emailed copy of it from her.

We also had a terrible experience with Selorm and Effia about Etse. We needed some information from Caleb's birth family and we no longer trusted Selorm or Effia to translate for us. Victory contacted the twin's grandfather and asked him to come to our house for a private talk. Then Victory acted as our translator. We told the twin's grandfather that we wanted him to take Etse and Peace back to his home. We told him we would send enough money to help him and his wife take care of them, and that we would provide funds for him to start his own business so his income would increase and become sustainable. He said that he would think about our offer and let us know.

Just when we had been about to start conversing with the grandfather, one of the older boys from Last Hope showed up. We didn't want him around but he insisted he was there to guide the grandfather back to his village. That was ridiculous because the man had travelled to our place quite fine on his own. Then I realized that the directors must have received word that the grandfather was here with us. The boy was sent to spy on our meeting. If we made the boy leave and return to Last Hope there undoubtedly would have been consequences for him. He was just an innocent pawn being used by Selorm and Effia, so we let him stay, knowing full well we'd hear from them sometime soon.

Right on cue, about thirty minutes after the grandfather and the boy left our house, Selorm called me on my cell. She went on a screaming rampage for five minutes. The directors were furious that we had talked to the grandfather privately. I held the cell phone at arm's length from my ear while Selorm yelled and yelled about how terrible we were to speak with him behind their backs.

The next morning they called and insisted we go to Last Hope to have a meeting with them. It was hotter than most days and when we arrived, they were sitting outside under the shade of a tree. Etse was the only child outside. He was standing in the hot sun and looked like the heat was starting to get the best of him. All the other children were inside watching TV, where it was cooler. Effia and Selorm told us that Etse was hungry and would not go inside with the rest of the children. My mom and I immediately became suspicious. The whole scene felt like it was staged.

Next, the directors told us they had run out of money and had not been able to feed the children for the last two days (why is it always two days?!). Just then, an ice-cream vendor passed in front of their compound. Selorm called to a girl who was watching TV and instructed her to go and bring back cold treats for the four of us. We objected that it was cruel to buy treats for just the adults. Effia shrugged and then insisted that the girl go and buy treats for just her and Selorm. Selorm handed the girl enough money to run after the vendor and buy whatever it was the two of them wanted.

Can you believe they kept haranguing us to give them money while they sat there and ate their ice-cream? Even though we have repeatedly told them we cannot use our money to support the place that has housed Caleb prior to his adoption, they kept imploring us to give them money. They have been doing this to us throughout our stay and it is wearing both my mom and I out. They know we will not jeopardize our adoption, but they keep at it, telling us we are whites, and we should be grateful they gave Caleb to us, so now we should help all the children. Then they called Etse over and asked him to take his shirt off so we could see how much weight he had lost since he'd been living at Last Hope. Etse had not acknowledged us since we'd arrived, and he just stood there with a sullen expression on his face.

He did look thinner and when Selorm asked him if he was hungry, he said yes. Effia asked Etse to tell us if he had enough food to eat every day. Etse looked at Selorm and then looked down at his feet. A moment passed, and then he muttered that he never had enough food to eat and he was always hungry, so we should give money to Selorm. The whole thing was completely disingenuous and there was no mistaking that Etse was their pawn. We hated to see them using him like that.

My mom motioned to me to walk away from them so we could talk in private. She pointed out what I knew but could not stomach. As long as these two women were in charge, Etse will always be hungry, or sick, or have some sort of emergency need for money. I was insistent that we call a spade a spade. We marched back over to the directors and told them unequivocally, that they could not use Etse to blackmail us, and that we were thoroughly disgusted with their actions. They were none too pleased with our reaction.

We won't let Charity and Caleb go to Last Hope anymore. Victory came over later in the day and we told her what had happened. She reminded us that Etse is doing much better at Last

Hope even if the food is not as nutritious as what we fed him. She agreed that if we gave in once to their demand for money, they would continue to use Etse as their pawn, over and over again.

Like us, Victory desperately hopes the grandfather will take us up on our offer. We all know Etse and Peace will be better off back in their village with their grandparents and other relatives, but we cannot force him into caring for them.

Victory is the one that educates us on the 'real deal' with Ghanaian orphanages. She says it is common practice for owners of orphanages in Ghana to coerce parents into giving them legal custody of their children because parents are persuaded that their children will receive a better education. Only five or so children at Last Hope were literally orphans and truly parentless. The rest of the children, forty of them, had parents or adult relatives living nearby who paid a fee to have their child housed at Last Hope. All those parents shared the same hope—that their child would be exposed to whites and perhaps even adopted by a white and taken to another country for a better life and education. They believed that their child would then, in the future, be able to support the rest of their family back in Ghana when he or she entered the job market. Paying to house your child at a place like Last Hope was like buying a lottery ticket. You didn't stand a chance of winning if you didn't buy a ticket, and placing your child in one of these so called orphanages was the equivalent of buying a lottery ticket. Orphanages are a business enterprise, and Effia and Selorm are masters at welcoming volunteers, offering them outstanding hospitality and staging things at Last Hope. They both exude warmth, kindness and a sense of family to draw volunteers in emotionally. It's done to optimize the probability that whites will become enamored with a child or with the enterprise as a whole. In their eyes, opening white hearts equates to opening white wallets. Last Hope was not created from a foundation of compassionate, social responsibility. It is as much an entrepreneurial enterprise as any of the various shops in the villages or cities. From these conversations, I now believe that the directors of Last Hope viewed volunteers and visitors as potential money trees that they could assertively shake down for money over and over again. When I returned home from my first trip, Effia and Selorm repeatedly emailed or phoned me, pleading for money to cover one emergency after another. A particular child had fallen sick, or all the children were without food, or they needed new uniforms or new shoes or school tuition—it was always something like that, and it was endless. Most volunteers I stayed in contact with experienced the same thing, and regardless of reasons given for why funds were desperately needed, monies sent to the orphanage were never enough. But I want to stress that I was, at that time, happy to send whatever I could. I am just now more aware of the funds being used for other than what they were requested for and there is no accountability to funds being sent.

Cannot one small part of our plan work out? I just received an email from my supervisor at work. There have been cutbacks and everyone on leave must return or their positions may be dissolved. I will have to fly back home in two weeks when my mom leaves. Charity is a treasure. We don't know how we ever managed without her. We are going to spend the next two weeks preparing her to take care of Caleb. Victory and Hubert are going to keep a close eye on them for us. Thank goodness, we've already taught Charity so much about how to cook nutritious meals. She's been doing all the meal planning, shopping and cooking for us for the past month. She is always happy and she is so wonderful with Caleb whenever she teaches him or plays with him. It was never our plan to leave Caleb in anyone else's care but now we have no choice. If we had a choice, we would still choose Charity to be his caregiver, so thank goodness we have her.

We need to purchase lots of school supplies for Caleb and more clothes for both of them. Charity understands that neither she, nor Caleb, should ever go to Last Hope again, and she is fine with that. My parents have decided to sponsor her to come to Canada. She will stay with us for six months, then go to college and start a new life in Canada. We've begun the process of getting her a passport and we've sent off all the necessary paperwork to sponsor her. She is very excited about this.

Charity needs a bank account before she can apply for a passport. We need to go to Accra and arrange some banking details for her. We've worked out a generous budget for her and Caleb to remain in our house and eat well while we are gone. We have no idea how long it will be before they can get visas and leave Ghana.

The only anxiety we have is that my mom and dad had to make Effia their legal representative for Caleb now that I have to leave Ghana. Charity is not old enough to appoint, and Victory and Hubert did not qualify because they have not known Caleb long enough. We are caught between a rock and a hard place and have no other options. It is terrible to be in this situation; Effia and Selorm wouldn't even be on our B List of candidates, but our hands are tied. The only good news in all of this is that when we went to Accra to file the papers concerning Caleb's legal representative, the court also assigned us a court assistant to help us submit all the paperwork to the Canada High Commission Office here in Ghana. That is a huge relief to us because it means we don't need Effia to do anything for us and therefore she won't be able to interfere in any way. Basically, at this point, she is just a name on a paper.

Victory and Hubert are very sad that my mom and I need to leave soon. We have all become very close friends. We are sad to leave our wonderful neighbor, Henri, as well. I don't think he will ever understand how much his patio socials have meant to us. They have been our saving grace after many days that were fraught with frustration. My mom has decided to fund his house girl's education, so Charity went with us to the school, to act as our translator, while my mom paid for a whole year of the young teen's tuition.

Our thoughts are constantly with Caleb. He is so innocent and trusting. He knows I left once and came back for him. He knows he is now part of the Rondeau family and understands that we will be waiting for him back in Canada. Things went so smoothly at the adoption hearing we have new optimism that it won't be too long before we are all reunited again on Canadian soil. Nevertheless, it is going to be extremely difficult to leave Caleb behind again. Thank goodness, this will be the last time I ever have to leave Ghana without him! At least we know he has a wonderful person to care for him in the meantime.

Through all that has happened here in this little village, I do want to make one more effort at Last Hope. I purchase a mango tree and plant it in the front yard at Last Hope. With the way things grow here, it won't be long before the children will have fresh fruit to pick and maybe even remember us as having planted it there for them.

Victory and Hubert and going to drive all of us to the airport—so we will never have to ride in a trotro again. They are so thoughtful. Hubert suggested we all go out for dinner near the airport. We laughed and talked and had such a wonderful time. They made us all forget what would be happening in just a short while. After dinner, we all walked together the rest of the way to the airport terminal. As we are walking, again Victory and Hubert take the lead role and talk to Caleb about all the great things he will be doing while the Government completes the paperwork and that it will be very soon and they will be bringing him back to the airport to fly to Canada. We reach the doors and start to hug and kiss everyone goodbye, with lots of extra hugs and kisses for Caleb. But you can't loiter at the doors and the security guard comes by and tells everyone to move along. In just half a second our little party breaks up and goes our separate ways. It all happened so fast.

Fast forward and we are back on Canadian soil! We surprised everyone when we were able to get an earlier flight home. We only told Cody, so everyone else was completely surprised. We are very happy to be back in our lovely home and enjoy all the luxuries we take for granted—like hot running water. It was very hard to leave Caleb and Charity, but we are hopeful they will join us in the next couple of months. We miss them terribly even though we talk to them almost every day.

Third Trip

September – December 2009

As my parents' legal representative, Effia still needed to complete some work for us in regards to the adoption. At the time we asked her if she would do this part, we indicated to her that she cannot receive any compensation for this work. We would cover all costs, such as travel and accommodation expenses when Caleb's family had to go to Accra to be interviewed by Canada Immigration. She understood and agreed to do it under those terms. Bringing Caleb's family members to Accra, and taking Caleb to get his medical examination for his visa, was all we needed Effia to do for us. The same court assistant, who had assisted us through the adoption process, was assigned to us again to take care of all other legalities.

Before we left Ghana, we had purchased a modem and a prepaid Internet usage plan for Effia so she could stay in touch with us by email. We also purchased an ample amount of phone cards for her so she could call us at any time, but email was our primary mode of communication with them.

We felt we needed to keep in touch with Ghana in many different ways in order to come to our own conclusion on how things were going. I did my part by chatting online with many volunteers who had worked at one of the other Children's Homes in Anagonyigba. During their work-term, volunteers would drop in at Last Hope for a visit or simply see some of the children from Last Hope as they would be walking back and forth to their school in Anagonyigba. It was always obvious when Last Hope had not attracted volunteers for a while because I would be told that the children looked unkempt, dirty or even sickly. Then, when other volunteers actually did a work term at Last Hope, the children's care would improve. We now knew that during those times, it wasn't that the two operating directors of Last Hope had a change of heart and wanted to give better care to their wards. The level of care the children received improved during those times because it was inextricably tied in with their business marketing strategy. The children were pawns, used for the benefit of Effia and Selorm's business.

After the first three to four weeks of tri-weekly phone calls with Caleb, I noticed that he sounded different and I could tell something was bothering him. Even though I tried to get him to tell me what was bothering him, he wouldn't—of course in hindsight I realized he could not talk freely to me because Charity would have been standing right beside him during those calls. At that time though, all I could do was ask Charity if something was bothering Caleb. All she replied was that she was having trouble with the directors of Last Hope. Though I pressed her for specifics, she wouldn't elaborate. We emailed our friend Victory and asked her to look in on them. She emailed back that Charity had heard that the directors had cursed her and Caleb. Charity believed in voodoo and Victory thought that perhaps

Charity was scaring Caleb by sharing her fears about being cursed. Victory went to talk with Charity to assuage her fears and didn't think the situation called for any more action than that.

It was only later, much later in hindsight that we remembered that the children in the compound of our rental house had told us that Charity washed fish bones behind our house. We had no idea what that meant at the time, or why the children had informed us about it. When we returned to Canada, we searched online and realized it was an act of voodoo meant to harm us. The kids had been trying to warn us of her.

In mid-October we finally received notification from the High Commission Office in Accra that a date, October 27, had been set to interview Caleb's mother and grandmother. This appointment was to confirm that both women understood that Caleb would be leaving Ghana to live in Canada. If they couldn't get to Accra for October 27, they had sixty days to appear. This was one of the tasks Effia had agreed to do for us as Caleb's legal representative, so of course we tried to contact her to confirm she would do it. We also needed Effia to contact Victory to pick up the money we'd be sending to cover all the travel expenses for Effia and the other two women.

My mom had arranged with Victory before we left that all money being sent over to assist with Caleb's care and the final steps for the adoption would come to her. We did not want to send money directly to Selorm or Effia because we did not trust them to use it for its intended purpose. Victory portioned out our money to

Charity each month for housing expenses, travel, food and wages. Victory would also give money to Effia to cover the expenses she would incur during the upcoming trip to the High Commission Office in Accra. We felt we could trust Victory to let us know if the costs that Effia was quoting were in alignment with what the 'real' costs were.

Unfortunately, this process wasn't acceptable to Effia and I received this email from Charity:

Please about the money you want to send, I think you send it to Effia instead of Victory, because Effia asked me if you will be sending money and I told her you will sent it through Victory and she got mad and was saying that if you send the money through Victory then she will not let Caleb, his mother and his grandmother go for the interview, to make Effia happy I think you send the money to her.

When Effia found out we were going to stick to our plans and send money through Victory, she refused to answer our calls or our emails. Then we heard from our court assistant that Charity's birth certificate had arrived with the wrong date of birth on it. Effia had taken that copy of Charity's birth certificate, and promised that she would go to the registry office in Anagonyigba to apply for a corrected version, but she kept making excuses and procrastinating, so that task had yet to be completed.

It was very hard to tell what was going on in Ghana. Even though we had asked Charity to stay in the village and to seek out Victory if she needed help, she refused to do so. Then one day

Charity emailed us and said that she had taken Caleb back to her apartment in Accra because something wasn't working in our rental house. We found out later that Effia and Selorm had ordered her to teach at Last Hope and to bring Caleb with her every day, so she did as she was told for a week and then took Caleb back to her apartment in Accra. Without us there, Charity seemed to obey Effia and Selorm more than us. We found out later that Charity had actually grown up in the same household as Selorm. They were cousins that were raised like sisters, even though Selorm was much older. No one had disclosed that to us when we interviewed Charity for her position. Selorm was a formidable woman and Charity would have had to do her bidding or face some type of consequence. Remember too, that Charity believed in voodoo, so any further threat of curses directed towards her would probably have been enough to get her to follow their orders.

We tried to speak with Victory to ask what was going on, but, like us, Victory hoped that Caleb's visa would be issued sooner than later. At this time we didn't know that there was going to be a major delay processing his visa. Victory is a wise and compassionate woman. She said she elected not to tell us because she knew it would have been difficult to hear of it when we were helpless to do anything about it. Our only hope was to keep a line of communication open with Charity for Caleb's sake. We also hoped that Effia would eventually contact us about her insistence to have the money for travel expenses sent directly to her. We were anxious to get Caleb's mother and grandmother to Accra for their interview, so that requirement in Caleb's visa application could be fulfilled.

Getting those interviews completed wasn't our only challenge. Caleb also needed to undergo a medical exam that could only be done by certain doctors who have contracts with the High Commission Office in Accra. Then, the High Commission Office informed us that we also needed the Ghanaian Department of Social Welfare (DSW) to fill out a special form granting permission for Caleb to leave the country. This was news to us as none of our paperwork had cited this requirement. My mom asked the DSW to email that form to us so we could forward it to our court assistant in Ghana. Even though we stressed that the paper copy of the form should NOT be mailed to Effia, they mailed it to her anyway.

So now, Effia is holding all the trump cards in her hand. She has the special medical forms, the form that the DSW needed to fill out, she can decide to take the mother and grandmother to the interview or not, and she also has Charity's birth certificate that we need for her passport.

There is nothing further we can do from Canada, except...wait.

Charity kept calling to tell us she was out of money and needed more to be able to take care of Caleb. We sent her a couple more hundred dollars through Victory, but told Charity she needed to email us a list of her expenses because the budget we had worked out for her was enough to feed and care for a family of four. In other words, Charity was now blatantly trying to get more money out of us and we couldn't help but wonder if Effia and Selorm were pressuring her to do so. We kept instructing Charity to ask Effia to contact us directly about all the paperwork that needed to be done. Next Charity told us that Effia could not contact us herself because she had become very sick. Finally in early November, Effia finally contacted us and demanded money from us. When we asked her to state the amount of money she wanted, she told us that we knew how things worked in Africa, and should be able to figure it out ourselves. And then hung up on us. We knew what it cost to travel from Anagonyigba and back, to stay overnight in Accra, to eat in restaurants and to dash everyone, including the police officers at the road checkpoints. We tallied up the expenses and decided to send her twice that amount. Then we waited to find out her reaction. To our relief she took Caleb's mother and grandmother for their interview in Accra but afterwards, once again, she refused to communicate with us. About a month later Charity called my mom.

It was with an urgency that had not been there before. She told her that the directors wanted GH¢40,000 cedis. My mom decided to play dumb and pretend that she understands they must need more money by now to replenish their supply of phone cards. This is why everyone in Ghana almost never calls my mom. She had trouble the whole trip with trying to understand what people were saying because of their thick accent. It is also in part her personality, if she doesn't want to be specific about something she puts on this bewildered act. Just ask her for directions to somewhere sometime—you will see what I mean. Right now, this is working in our favor. You see, Ghana has an old currency that some people still use when they speak about amounts of money. She decides to pretend that she means 40,000 of the old currency, which would be the same as GH¢40 cedis ($32 CAD). That was an adequate amount of money to purchase more phone cards even though she knew perfectly well they had not used up the other phone cards with phone calls to us. Anyway, she tells Charity she will send GH¢40 cedis to Victory to give to Effia. Charity pleaded with her not to do that and insisted that Effia and Selorm would not touch any money that came through Victory. My mom also asks if Charity is still in Accra with Caleb and she says she is.

We are still in the midst of trying to find out if our rental house is in fact uninhabitable. We don't make an issue of it with Charity because we needed to keep her talking with us. But my mom doesn't like them in Accra. So she tells Charity that we want her to bring Caleb to Victory's house in Anagonyigba. She also tells her that we are not going to use Effia as our legal representative anymore. Charity becomes hysterical. She tells my mom that Effia had told her to make it very clear to us, that if we tried to change who our legal representative was, Effia would make certain that Caleb would never leave Africa with us. It is now becoming very obvious to us that Charity had been coached as a 'middle man' to try and extort money from us on behalf of the two operating directors of Last Hope.

We knew then, that we had to get Caleb away from Charity. My mom kept phoning her, asking her to bring Caleb to Victory's house in Anagonyigba. She was also phoning Victory to ensure she would take Caleb in and also get her assistance to get Charity to take Caleb to her. We were terrified that the directors would take Caleb and disappear with him. Accra is a city of millions and it would be impossible for us to track him down. Then Charity told us that she couldn't move Caleb anywhere because he was sick with malaria. Victory began calling Charity too, to persuade her to bring Caleb to her so Victory could take him to the hospital. We told Charity that if she just did the right thing at this point, we could work something out with the directors and still give her an opportunity to come to Canada.

We believed that Charity was being used and we thought that after we got Caleb to safety, we could try to get Charity away from the directors' influence. Victory agreed to let Charity stay with them if she showed up with Caleb. Their housing compound was heavily guarded and only invited guests were let in through a locked gate. Effia and Selorm wouldn't be able to approach Charity or Caleb once they were inside the compound. Our anxiety felt like it would suffocate us. We waited and waited for the phone to ring, hoping it was Victory telling us Caleb was finally with her. Both my mom and I just kept dialing Charity's cell phone over and over again. We wouldn't let up—we couldn't give up—Caleb needed to be safe.

Finally, my mom got through to Charity and kept talking with her, pleading with her, and promising her everything would be worked out once she got to Victory's house. Later that day, Victory called my mom. Charity had arrived with Caleb and she'd agreed to stay there and not leave the compound. I can't tell you how relieved she was to talk with Caleb for a few minutes. Victory had already taken him to the hospital because he did in fact have early symptoms of malaria but had bounced back very quickly once he received medication. He still wasn't talking openly but he told her he really liked being there because he could play with Baby Sam a little bit.

My mom and I decided it was critical for her to go back to Ghana. We were sure that once word got back to Effia and Selorm that Charity and Caleb were in Anagonyigba again, they would try to find some way to take Caleb and disappear with him. The next morning we went to the Ghanaian High Commission Office in Edmonton and discussed our fears with the director. At first he claimed our story was preposterous, but we insisted tenaciously that it was true. Finally, he admitted that such things were possible in Ghana. My mom wanted to fly back to Ghana but he would not grant her a visa. He was afraid that once she had Caleb in her custody again, she might choose to stay in Ghana and live a life in hiding if Caleb's visa was denied. In other words, he believed a mother would not be able to leave her son behind if his visa was denied. He told me I was a better candidate for obtaining a visa because I had already travelled there and returned twice.

By the next morning, I had my visa and even though there was a freak snow storm, my mom got me to my flight on time. I was met at the Accra airport in Ghana by people whose identity we have to protect at all costs. They drove me back to their house where I spent the night. The next day I anxiously waited until 3 pm before I heard Victory, Hubert, Sam, Charity and of course, Caleb arrive.

As soon as Caleb spotted me, he screamed in delight and jumped into my arms. He buried his face in my neck and kept hugging me. Charity was dumbfounded with shock and surprise because Victory had not said a word to her about me returning to Ghana, but she recovered quickly and acted happy to see me. Caleb looked like he had lost weight and he stuck to me like glue which was more than fine because it felt so good to be able to hug him again.

I called my mom and our whole family was incredibly relieved to hear that I had Caleb, literally, in my arms. But we still had the challenge of retrieving the important documents that were in Effia's possession; the medical forms and the form for the Department of Social Welfare to fill out. We had been trying unsuccessfully to get new copies of them emailed to us, but time was ticking by and nothing was happening, so Victory managed to persuade Effia to rendezvous with her in Accra to give the forms to her.

The rendezvous was slated for the next morning. Charity must have texted Effia that I had come back to Ghana because when I went with Victory to get the documents, Effia acted like she had been expecting me. She ignored Victory, and just strode up to me and slapped a large envelope into my hand. I was expecting some kind of dramatic reaction, and I got more than I bargained for.

At first she didn't say a word. She puffed herself up, shoved her face into mine and then just glowered at me with an intimidating expression. Then she said, "Here's your papers!" in a very menacing way. Her tone of voice was sending me the unspoken message of, "You better watch your back!" Then she stomped off. It was over quite quickly.

Victory had made an appointment with a doctor that could do Caleb's medical exam for his visa, so we went there immediately after Effia left us. Once that was completed, we headed back to Victory and Hubert's place in Anagonyigba. It is the place where we feel safest because their compound is well guarded around the clock.

I phone home to my mom and let her know where we are and I also talk to her about my concerns that Charity is acting as an informant for Effia. My mom doesn't want to believe it. She had bonded with Charity and she is looking for excuses for Charity's behavior. But my mom is on the other side of the world and I am here in the flesh.

I am wary and watchful. Charity is being noticeably persistent about quickly coming over to stand near Caleb each time he attempts to talk to me. He shrinks away from her and drops his voice to a whisper each time she does this, so it was becoming clear to me that he felt threatened by her. Victory took it upon herself to give Caleb and me some much needed privacy. Charity assumed that she would continue to sleep in the same guest room with Caleb and me, as we did in Accra, but as soon as we arrived at Victory and Hubert's house, Victory directed Charity to sleep in a smaller room, typically assigned to a house girl. Victory had not yet hired another house girl to replace the previous one, who hated to do any work, so the room was vacant.

Charity became very upset over this sleeping arrangement, but Victory insisted and Charity had to respect her wishes. Now Caleb and I finally have some much needed time together. He has his bedtime shower and cuddles with me and talks and talks and talks, as if he has been bottling stuff up and now needs to get it all out at once. He tells me about being taken back to Last Hope every day and forced to go to school there again. Charity would cane him and call him a bad boy every day. She stopped feeding him the foods we had instructed her to prepare for him and often fed him the same thing over and over again for days. Sometimes, she withheld food from him completely, telling him that we were not sending enough money for him to eat every day.

Caleb had been very frightened when she took him to Accra because he didn't know anyone and didn't speak the regional dialect there. Every morning Charity would take him to a small shop and instruct him to sit on a chair until she came back. He then had to wait hours and hours, and it was always dark before she would return. Then, Charity would send him out into the unfamiliar neighborhood to buy charcoal for her. You cannot imagine how horrified I was to hear all of this. And I was furious—incredibly furious that Charity had sent this little six year old boy out into a strange neighborhood at night. He told me he had to follow strangers and ask many, many people to help him find the charcoal shop.

The next morning, I make no mention of Caleb's stories. There are still lots of things that need to get done to get us out of Ghana. I had brought a new authorization form with my mom and dad's signatures that would grant me legal, temporary custody of Caleb until he arrived home in Canada. Charity overhears Victory and me as we make plans for me to go to the Department of Social Welfare (DSW) in Accra to submit a report about Effia and Selorm's threat to kidnap Caleb. Charity looked as if she had seen a ghost. She asked me how I knew of the directors' plan to kidnap Caleb. I reminded her that she had told my mom about it over the phone. Charity became very flustered and insisted she had not been the one to reveal that to my mom. When she continued to vehemently deny what she had done, I went back to my room and brought out the letter that my mom and dad had written to the DSW; the one I was going to submit on their behalf when I registered a legal complaint against Effia and Selorm.

I showed the letter to Charity and read it out loud to her. She argued that she had revealed that information to my mom in confidence and that my mom was rude for sharing their conversation with others. I couldn't believe what I was hearing. Charity turned around and abruptly left the room. I was just about to go after her when Victory's phone rang. As she listened to whoever it was, her expression told me that whatever she was hearing was causing her great concern. She hung up and looked around to make sure we were alone. Then she told me, in a whisper, what the call was about.

The caller was a well-known, local priest. He had asked Victory if she had taken a child to the hospital recently. She didn't want to mention anything about Caleb. She told the priest her baby, Sam had been quite ill and they'd spent a lot of time at the hospital in recent weeks. Then he had asked her if she had taken a young boy there too, the one who was adopted by the white women in Anagonyigba. When she admitted she had, the priest then asked her if a young woman had been taking care of the child and Victory confirmed that that was indeed the case. Next, the priest asked Victory if we still planned to bring the girl to Canada with us. Obviously, after Caleb's disclosures, we were not, and the priest must have heard the hesitation in Victory's voice when she didn't say yes immediately. The priest then told Victory there was now a plot to murder Caleb and that we needed to hide him somewhere safe immediately. He told her that the people who wanted Caleb dead were well connected, and he warned Victory that her family was also in danger. His last words were to trust no one.

I asked immediately if the priest said who had given him this information. Victory said that the priest would only say it was a young woman that had told him in a confidential way. We assume he means he had heard it during a confession.

Victory and I are both stunned and shocked. Victory asks me if I had told Charity she was no longer coming to Canada but I explained that the phone call had come just as I had been about to confront Charity. Then I realized that there was a chance Charity might already know as I suddenly had a flashback of a very short conversation that had occurred between us just hours before. My mom had bought Charity an iPod® with two chargers; one that worked in Ghana and one that would work in Canada. In my rush to pack, I had left my charger behind so I had asked Charity to give me the one that worked in Canada. I might have even said something along the lines of, "It doesn't make sense for you to have the Canadian one now." I'm not sure if those were the exact words I used, but whatever I said came with an inference that Charity no longer needed a charger that would work in Canada. I'm pretty sure that's when Charity knew she was staying in Ghana. Anyway, as I am relating this conversation to Victory, we were interrupted by Charity.

She bursts into the room and immediately begins accusing me of treating her poorly. She yells that she knew that we were not going to take her to Canada all along and that she didn't want to see me ever again. She already had a bunch of bags stacked by the door and she stomps out of the house with them. There is already a taxi waiting to pick her up so we knew her exit had been preplanned.

Charity must have realized that she had made a terrible mistake when she told my mom about the operating directors' threat to kidnap Caleb. She knew that once an official complaint against Effia was made, a copy of it would be sent to Last Hope. Charity knew that they would trace the leak back to her.

Caleb was the first child adopted from one of the three orphanages in Anagonyigba. It would bring the operating directors a tremendous amount of status if a child was successfully adopted by whites. They could brag about it for years and therefore persuade even more parents to sign their children over to them. If word got out that an official complaint had been filed against either of the directors of Last Hope, it would ruin their reputation. It had the potential to destroy their business in catastrophic ways and damage their connections with sources of volunteers and donations. Charity would be blamed for all this and she probably knew better than anyone else, what Effia and Selorm were capable of when so much was at stake.

In one day, the threat of kidnapping Caleb has escalated to a plan to murder him, and before I can even call my mom to talk about the events that have transpired, the day becomes even more dramatic.

After Charity stormed out, Victory and I were both relieved to have her gone. Victory suggested that we wait for Hubert to come home so we could discuss the priest's warning message and make a plan for Caleb and me to go into hiding. So now we wait.

Caleb is in the living room watching a movie on TV and I am in the kitchen with Victory helping to make the evening's dinner. I hear a knock at the front door and I hear Caleb walk over, open the door and then close it again and return to the living room. I just assumed one of the workers had needed to come into the entry way to get a key. None of the employees are allowed to carry their own set of keys. The keys were all kept in the entry way by the front door so they need to come inside to get a key or return a key. But next I hear voices yelling through an open living room window. I cannot believe my ears—it is Effia and Selorm ordering Atsu to open the front door for them.

I start freaking out and run into the living room and quickly shut all the windows. I don't want them anywhere near Caleb. Victory meets me in the entrance way with Baby Sam strapped to her back. She motions for the two of us to go outside immediately and confront them out there. When we immerge from the house, Effia and Selorm begin to yell at me, and both of them attempt to slap me and push me around. They yell that I had cheated them out of tons of money and that I was a greedy white who had never helped them in any way. They accuse my mom and me of lying to Charity about bringing her to Canada. Then they yell even louder that Caleb is theirs, and that they will make sure we never get him out of Ghana alive.

It is a very physical altercation. It is hard for me to hold my ground against the two of them. Then they do something weird. They begin to taunt me. They push me and then they challenge me to go to the police, to charge them with assault. They are doing this over and over. Finally, Victory pulls at me from behind to get me closer to the front door, and then she quickly opens it, pulls me inside, and slams the door in their faces. Then, thank goodness, they up and leave. Usually there are lots of guards around, but the compound is strangely empty except for the two exiting operating directors.

Once inside I immediately go over to Caleb and ask him if he is OK. He is watching a Harry Potter Movie. He looks up at me and after a slight hesitation, he tells me he is fine except that the movie is a little scary, but he quickly adds that he still likes it. That is an incredible moment for me and Caleb. Selorm and Effia had been outside acting extremely aggressive but Caleb had not become afraid of them. He is a little innocent boy who, in this particular moment, simply believes that I will protect him and keep him safe from them. It was a sign that our bond is deepening.

It's great that Caleb is fine. I am not. I am terrified. I need to talk to my mom. She isn't picking up the phone so I leave her around a dozen messages before she finally calls me back. After I tell her everything that has happened in the last day. She knows both

Caleb and I are both in serious danger, as is Victory's family. We both believe that after Effia and Selorm showed up at Victory's house and their remarks, that they are in fact 'the people' who want to murder Caleb.

In our opinion, it seems conceivable that even though Effia had agreed to help with the adoption, she may have believed that she would find a way to wrangle a significant amount of money out of us in one way or another. When we finally put our foot down and told them that we would absolutely not give another cent to Last Hope for any reason whatsoever, they finally got the message. If up to that point in time, Effia still had any thoughts of getting compensated for acting as the legal representative, they ended with that confrontation. Their two white money trees were off limits and they may have believed they could have shaken a lot more cash out of us, than they had up to that point in time.

Effia and Selorm were schemers and manipulators. Some people do go to African countries and pay tens of thousands of dollars in order to expedite an adoption. We were very clear from the start, that we would not be doing it that way. They must have had a plan, but they had never had a reason to understand the legalities of a private adoption, as this was the first of its kind in their village. Maybe it was due to the fact that they were so accustomed to offering bribes to side-step legalities and open any door that was locked by the legal system, that they were now faced with a new situation they had never encountered. Suddenly their two whites were not cooperating with their Plan A, which they thought would yield them big bucks. And we are just getting an inkling of their Plan B and it doesn't seem to be in our favor for certain!

I truly believe that power, control and money are everything to them. We had unknowingly interrupted a system that had been in place for a long time, one that had consistently greased the palms of many people. Obviously, Effia and Selorm still believed Caleb was a commodity of theirs, and the closer we came to leaving the country with their commodity, the closer they came to losing their final chance to cash in on Caleb's adoption. These women were by no means going to simply stand by and become idle spectators as events unfolded.

I think, too, that greed kept them fixated and short sighted on the prize in front of them. Caleb was their prize child who had attracted rich white people to adopt him. We aren't rich by any means, but from their perspective, we were. He was living proof that their business plan was working and in a sense he was a huge cash cow. I think they viewed the entire experience as a win-lose situation. The more their realization grew that their prize child was slipping through their fingers, the more extreme measures they took to try and regain possession of him. We were getting very close to flying Caleb out of the country. Selorm and Effia each had a dark side that was malevolent, angry and vengeful and therefore capable of anything. Throughout our entire experience with them, control was extremely important to them. There was a cultural issue about us being their whites, and we, naively, didn't give enough thought to what that really meant. I think that at this point in time, with Caleb reunited with me, and Charity no longer in charge of him, others may have viewed the two operating directors as being less powerful with respect to their whites, and that may have had future consequences for them. Status was everything. Money was everything, and control was everything. They were losing money and control, so status would have been intrinsically lost too. In a culture of dashing and bribery, people with the most power get paid more before it trickles down to everyone below them in status. When the situation appeared to get more and more beyond their control, it seems to have really pissed them off in ways we could never have imagined.

My mom is super busy making phone calls to our local Member of Parliament (MP), and asking them what can be done. She calls friends that have connections to other African countries to see if she can find a safer place for us. Caleb still didn't have a visa, so we can't go to Canada, but she thinks that perhaps there were other countries we might be able to flee to.

I'm worried that at this point the Ghanaian government still have Effia listed as Caleb's legal representative. I want my mom to find out what rights she may have over me at this point. Maybe that's why she wanted me to go to the police. I know I leave my mom with a million questions and almost as many things to look into when I end our conversation—she has my dad for support and is a very strong and determined woman. I admire her strength in times when any of us kids have needed her all through our lives. She will figure things out.

Hubert arrived home shortly after I spoke with my mom and he was furious with his security men for letting those two women into his compound. He was extremely concerned about the situation. He told me to pack up our things. Victory had previously arranged for all the items we had bought for Caleb during our three month stay to be brought from the rental house in Anagonyigba to her home. When I went to pack them up, everything was gone. Charity had taken it all with her; the books, toys, movies, school supplies—everything!

My mom calls me back. She has received an anonymous call. She has no idea who it was. She has spoken to so many people in the Canadian government and leads into people that could be of possible help in Ghana. The caller told her to warn me not to go to the police station and register an official assault charge against the operating directors. The caller told her that Effia and Selorm had already gone to the police to accuse me of kidnapping Caleb from Last Hope. There was now a warrant out for my arrest! I needed to stay out of sight. If I was arrested, it would take a while for everything to get sorted out, because Effia was still Caleb's legal representative—we were still waiting for the official notification that the legal transfer had been made from Effia to me. We both came to the same conclusion—we'd never see Caleb again if I was arrested and he was put back in Effia's custody.

When I hang up with my mom, and talk to Victory and Hubert about what she said, we were all very upset. However, it certainly explained why Effia and Selorm had tried to goad me, over and over again, to go to the police and charge them with assault. They had hoped I'd go there and conveniently for them—get arrested. Now we knew that I couldn't risk travelling anywhere by car or trotro, because I'd be spotted at one of the police checkpoints, but Hubert told me he had a plan, and he started to make phone calls to pull it together. After he was done on the phone, he excused himself and went out the door to speak with his security guards. He found out which guard had accepted a bribe from Effia and Selorm, and immediately turfed him off the property. Hubert was very irate. I don't know what he said to his guards but he did a lot of yelling. Then he came back inside and told Victory and me that he was calling in some reinforcements for his security team. Next, he and Victory spoke alone for a few minutes and then they came to me and explained what the plan was for Caleb and I to reach safety.

Hubert had made arrangements for Caleb and me to hide in a house in Accra. First we would need to get there safely, but for now, we were all going to stay overnight right where we were. Hubert assured us that we would be well guarded this time. He wasn't going to let any harm come to his wife, his infant son, Caleb or me. Then he explained his plan to get us to the hiding place in Accra.

Hubert travelled through the police checkpoints along the road to Accra dozens of times a week. He was so well known, he always got waved through. No one bothered to check his ID anymore, and they always waved his supply truck full of liquor through because he dashed very generously. The plan was for Hubert to drive the road to Accra at his regular time the next morning. His liquor supply truck would follow a few minutes behind him. If anyone had tipped off the police that I was trying to travel to Accra with Caleb to get us on a flight out of Ghana, the most likely place to hide us would be inside the truck, hidden out of sight behind stacks of crated liquor bottles. If the police pulled the truck over to search it at any of the checkpoints, it would indicate someone had tipped them off.

I know from talking to my mom, she wasn't going to sleep until I called her when we arrived in Accra. I, however, was so emotionally exhausted I actually fell asleep soon after I put Caleb to bed. I trusted Hubert completely and if he said we were safe, I knew he meant it. He loved his family and would never do anything to jeopardize their safety. The next morning Hubert drove to Accra. His car was waved through all the checkpoints, but his truck was stopped and searched thoroughly, so we knew the police had been tipped off. Hubert drove to all his normal places in Accra as if it was just another typical day and then he drove back to Anagonyigba.

Once Hubert's empty liquor truck returned to Anagonyigba we hoped the police at the checkpoints would assume Caleb and I were not attempting to travel to Accra by car. Hubert's car had windows that were darkly tinted. The only chance we had to get to somewhere safe to hide, was for Caleb and me to hide in the back seat as he drove through the checkpoints for a second time that day. All we could do was hope and pray his car wouldn't be searched. It was an all or nothing risk. We needed Lady Luck on our side or I would be arrested and we'd lose Caleb forever.

Hubert, Victory and Baby Sam sat in the front seat of the car. Caleb and I climbed into the back of Hubert's car. It was later in the day and it was just getting dark.

This is unquestionably the most terrifying experience of my life. I'm lying flat on the floor in the back seat of Hubert's car, hoping the tinted windows will offer the invisibility we desperately need. I've pushed Caleb almost completely under the front seat thinking if the check point police discover me, maybe they'd be so satisfied with arresting me they wouldn't think to search for him. It sounds all too ludicrous, but I'm a willing recipient of wishful thinking spawned from a place of sheer desperation. Hubert is doing a great job of chatting with them as if this were any other daily crossing he makes for his business. His wife, Victory, is sitting in the front passenger seat with baby Sam. Thank God he is so well known to them. I hold my breath the whole time they talk, right until I hear his foot switch to the gas pedal and feel the car pulling away. I place a fake confident smile on my face for the precious little brown face peering at me with huge questioning almond shaped dark eyes, but I feel sick to my stomach with a mixture of emotions. I am incredibly relieved that our plan has worked so far, but I still have gut twisting fear that we won't be entirely safe until we make it through airport security and board a plane for home. I'm worried sick they'll find us at the safe house that we are travelling to and snatch him from me – vanishing with him forever, or worse, kill him like the priest warned us they would do. I can't let that happen – not ever, but I feel so outnumbered! I think Hubert must have told us we could get off the floor and sit up in the back seat again three times before we finally do. My heart is pounding so loud it is hard for me to hear him. Thank God for Hubert and Victory. They had thought ahead and Hubert is handing each of us a cold can of soda. They must have known that at least I needed something to pour down my dry throat. Then I hear that sweet little voice ask me in a breathy whisper, "Mandi, do I talk now or whisper?" It felt so good to pull him into my lap for a cuddle. "You can talk all you want now. You were so good at being as quiet as a kitty." I say as brightly as I can, trying to inject normality back into the moment. "And I'll get to pet that kitty cat in your pictures when I get to Canada, right Mandi? And feed it every day, right?" he asks. "Yes you will my little nugget. You sure will!" Hubert winks at me in his rearview mirror and gives me a reassuring thumbs up. I try to take a deep breath but my lungs feel encased in cement from the fear. In a country of millions, there are only four people I can trust, and countless others who are happy to do the bidding of those who now, are willing to kill if that's what it will take to prevent the beautiful little boy sitting in my lap from reaching Canadian soil. When we finally reach Accra, I call my mom to see how she is doing and what she found out regarding finding us some assistance. She was desperately trying to get help at the Canadian end of things. She went to our MP's office, (Member of Parliament) and they directed her to call Canada Immigration while they tried to connect with their High Commission Office in Ghana. When she spoke to someone at our Canadian Immigration Office, they didn't believe her story. The employee told her she had been to Ghana, and it was a peaceful country where no one would orchestrate this type of harm or violence towards an innocent child. Finally, after doing her best to persuade her to put her bias aside and assist us in some way, she instructed her to advise me to go to the Canadian High Commission Office in Accra.

My mom had also contacted one of our close family friends that had strong ties in Nigeria. They were working together to try and find a way to fly us there with very secure protection. It was hard to believe that at this point Nigeria would be a safer bet than Ghana for us. In the end, we needed one of the papers we had already given to the Canadian High Commission Office in Accra in order to travel there, but after going there and asking for the paper back, they wouldn't even supply us with a copy, so that plan was swiftly abandoned.

We finally end up in a safe house in Accra. All I can really say is that it was located in a residential neighborhood and we were to stay indoors at all times. There was a TV to watch and some table games, so I spent hours and hours trying to occupy Caleb. He understood that we needed to stay hidden, but I chose not to discuss the details with him. However, he's so bright that he still picks up on the seriousness of our situation. My mom calls me back to tell me that the Canadian government would help me leave Ghana safely, but Caleb would have to stay behind. They could do nothing to acquire his visa faster. I told my mom that was not an option. I wasn't ready to give up yet. There had to be a way to get Caleb home with me, so I made arrangements to be driven to the Canadian High Commission Office. Let's just say it was one of the worst experiences of my life.

In the movies, embassies are portrayed as places of sanctuary. People are taken in and provided refuge until they can be safely transported back to their homeland. The way I was treated was as far from that as you can imagine. First, I had to wait in a public access waiting room for hours on end. I was terrified that the operating directors, or friends of theirs, would think to look for us there because it seemed like such a logical place for us to ask for help. I was so relieved when they finally ushered me into another inner waiting room, out of sight from the public waiting room. I waited there for over an hour, but at least this room was air-conditioned. Finally, I was ushered into a third room that resembled the type of visiting room one might expect if you had gone into a penitentiary to visit an inmate. There were high walled cubicles where two people could sit facing one another, separated by thick glass dividers. The thick glass had a small circle of holes that you had to bring your face really close to, in order to speak, and listen to the person on the opposite side of the glass. I remember thinking at that point that safety for Caleb and I was only minutes away because I assumed that I'd soon be able to explain our situation to a Canadian official working at our Canadian High Commission Office.

The employees were all Canadians, yet no one believed my story even though I had all kinds of documents with me; an official copy of the complaint I'd registered with the Ghanaian DSW, a copy of the letter that my mom and dad had written that documented the details of Effia's threat to kidnap Caleb, and of course all the documents of Caleb's legal adoption order. No one believed me and I was devastated by the reaction I got. They labeled my circumstances as a personal conflict that I had brought upon myself. People had threatened to kidnap, and now murder Caleb, and they called it a personal conflict—how much more personal can it get than when people threaten to kill an innocent child? But to have them chalk all that up to something I had brought upon myself was unimaginable. Next, they told me that until they received Caleb's medical report, no further action would be taken on his visa, therefore nothing could be done on our behalf with regard to our present 'circumstances'. I was stunned! I cannot tell you how let down I felt by my own country. When I get the chance to call my mom, she goes online to get details of what services the High Commission of Canada was supposed to provide to Canadian citizens from their offices in Ghana. From the list of general services they state, among other services, that they will assist in cases where the wellbeing or whereabouts of a Canadian is in question and help Canadians victimized abroad find local support or return home. But then she finds another site that states the services they don't offer and one of them is that they will not intervene in private legal matters. It seems like they considered my situation a private legal matter.

I am horrified that they refused to intervene, especially when a child's life was at stake, because they labeled our circumstance as a private legal matter. The least they could have done was investigate my story to some degree before they settled on that conclusion.

My mom is trying to help me understand Caleb is not yet a Canadian citizen; his status with the High Commission Office was in a grey zone between the black and white dictates of immigration laws. He needs a visa, and without one he is without the protection of our Canadian government. His medical report should have arrived at the High Commission Office in Accra by now, so I knew my next job was to track it down and find out what was causing the delay. That medical report was essentially Caleb's ticket home, as it was the only thing delaying his visa. There is nothing I can do but call the High Commission Office every day to ask if they have received Caleb's medical report yet, and my mom was calling them from Canada too.

The answer was always the same, the Office kept telling us they were still waiting to receive the doctor's medical report. Normally it was supposed to take just a few days. Incredibly, the reports go from Ghana to France to be processed, and then back to the High Commission Office in Accra. I'm assuming because all governments know better than to trust information out of Ghana. Even Obama in the address he gave during our previous trip here alluded to the idea that Ghana must implement better practices in order to have continued support from the USA. My mom finally tracked down the contact information of the office in France and got in touch with them to ask why it was taking so long. They told her they had received the envelope from the doctor's office where Caleb's exam had been done but the envelope had arrived with no report in it. It was just an empty envelope. We found out later that one of the employees who was responsible for ensuring the report got from the doctor's office to France was fired. Allegedly, this person accepted a bribe to remove and destroy Caleb's file from the envelope.

I reflect back to the day I took Caleb to get his medical exam done. It was the same day that Effia met us to hand over the special documents we needed; the ones that had been mailed to her. Shortly after we left the doctor's office with Caleb, Effia must have paid a visit to the same office. You see, weeks ago when we had first made plans with Effia to take Caleb to have this examination done in Accra, she told us what the fee would be to have it done. On the day of Caleb's appointment, as I went to pay for it, I was surprised to find out the actual fee was only half of what Effia had told us. I distinctly remember commenting to Charity and Victory that this was yet another example of how Effia was trying to milk us for more money in any way possible. Later that same day, soon after we arrived at Victory's house back in Anagonyigba, the doctor's office called me and the receptionist immediately began apologizing about quoting the wrong cost of the medical exam to my friend Effia.

I had no idea what they were talking about until they explained the whole incident to me. They told me Effia had come to their office later that morning, blaming them for giving her wrong information about the price of Caleb's exam. They told me Effia had said she was there on my behalf and was very, very angry with the staff for making it look like she had lied to her whites.

Only two people heard me make that comment about Effia trying to milk us for more money; Victory and Charity. Charity must have texted Effia after we left the doctor's office. Victory certainly would not have done so.

It all seems to be a weird set of coincidences that these three incidents occurred. Effia visited the office, the medical file vanished from its envelope, and later on, someone was fired for accepting a bribe—quite an interesting series of events if you ask me.

After a plethora of calls on my mom's end in Canada, the next thing I know, the doctor calls me and asks me to bring Caleb back for another exam. I can't even explain how nerve-racking it is to leave the safe house and go back to his office. But my mom eventually sways me by pointing out that Caleb's medical report was his ticket out of Ghana. So I make the decision to risk the trip. When the doctor finishes his examination and fills out the special forms, he asks me to watch as he places Caleb's report into an envelope, seals it and hands it to a waiting courier. This doctor clearly did not want to lose his contract with the High Commission Office and this was his way of showing me that he was being very careful to ensure that the envelope containing the medical report was leaving his office, this time intact.

Now, there is nothing left to do but wait. My mom keeps calling the Canadian Immigration Office in Canada to make sure they were tracking this copy of the medical report on its way to France. I keep calling the Ghanaian High Commission Office to see if it has arrived back from France. With nothing else to do but sit day after day in the safe house, I decide to take a chance and go back another time to the High Commission Office to see if I could find someone who might believe my story. All they did was get mad at me for involving the Canadian Immigration Office in Canada, but at least they assured me they would phone as soon as they received Caleb's medical report from their processing department in France.

Back to the safe house I go. It doesn't have Internet so my mom calls me every day and actually most days she calls me twice a day. I have Hubert and Victory to talk to locally by phone, but that was the only support I had. It was simply too risky to contact anyone else. The fewer people who knew where Caleb and I were staying, the better. I took a chance twice to go to a small Internet café that was nearby and connect by email with friends and my mom, but other than that I stayed inside with Caleb.

Caleb is such an amazing child. Throughout this whole ordeal he rarely complains about our circumstances, but every once in a while he mentions that he is afraid the directors would come and take him away from me. He is too scared to sleep alone so he sleeps in my bed. Victory and Hubert came to visit us a few times. They are incredible people and their support means so much. Caleb loves these times and is always happy to play with Baby Sam. Kindly, they bring us wonderful food to eat as well. All the rest of the time, Caleb and I just hang out and talk a lot. Hiding together like this is only bonding us together even more. If you have never lived in hiding for fear of your life, you will never understand this bond. It is deep and will never go away.

I know my friends and family are interested in the people who owned the safe house. Even my mom is asking questions about them. I don't want to tell anyone any details about them except to say that they carried on with their normal daily activities as best they can with two housebound guests there the entire time. We need to be very careful to protect their anonymity.

After I took Caleb back to the doctor's office to get his medical exam done again, my cell phone begins ringing a couple of times an hour, for twenty four hours a day. Someone must have spotted us and informed the operating directors of Last Hope, that we were somewhere in Accra. That thought terrified me, and the constant ringing of my cell phone kept me on edge day and night. I think of Effia and the clout and connections she had the day my mom and I lost our luggage at the airport. How she was able, through just a phone call, to get us to bypass security completely and walk right out the doors with four huge, stuffed hockey bags—without raising an eyebrow of an official. How many things Effia had done along the way with a couple of phone calls and it was as good as done. We have no idea who she knows or who she can bribe. It only took a bribe of GH¢5 cedis to give us complete security clearance at Ghana's international airport. She is like a huge spider who can cast a larger and larger web wherever she pleases. It was now my job to make sure Caleb and I did not get trapped in it, but at the same time, I didn't know where the web was, so it was very worrisome.

When I told my mom about the phone constantly ringing day and night, she urged me to shut it off. But I said I didn't want to risk missing a call from the High Commission Office or Victory and Hubert, whom we placed all our trust in. Hubert had arranged for this safe house. If for some reason, Caleb and I needed to be moved somewhere else, I wanted to be ready, so I keep my cell phone on around the clock and become accustomed to the ringing.

My mom wants to come to Ghana and she goes back to plead her case to the Ghanaian High Commission office in Edmonton, but it is too close to Christmas. It is closed over the holidays. She works with our travel agent, Mardy, to check the Consulate Office in Ottawa, but they are also closed. They say everyone leaves Ghana at Christmas time, no one wants to go there. We hear that you can take a chance and just fly to Ghana without a visa and that they would issue you one when you landed there—you only need to dash someone. My mom discusses the idea with Mardy, but apparently airlines could be heavily fined for carrying a passenger without a visa to a destination country. He told her if she left Canada without a Ghanaian visa, there was a very high risk that she'd be detained in Germany, where she'd have to switch planes.

Christmas Day comes and we are still in the safe house. This is so very, very difficult for me. My family has always been together for Christmas and I normally do the cooking. I love everything about Christmas and really miss my family. They call us, and everyone talks for hours, but in the end it just isn't enough. I want my family. I want us to be safe. I want to be home. We are all worried because Caleb and I have been hiding for over two weeks. Two weeks is an awful long time when you live it hour by hour and minute by minute. My mom tried to cheer me up by promising that we would do Christmas again when Caleb and I arrived home. This is such a low point. When we arrive home—what if we never arrive back home? I think I am going mad and all I can do is look at Caleb and draw him close for hugs and kisses. It's then that I know somewhere deep inside that we have to find a way to make it home to Canada. I just want to go home.

I just want my family. And I want Caleb with me when I do finally go back.

Two days after Christmas, my mom calls sooner than she usually does. I know something is up just through her voice. She tells me she just got off the phone with Charity. Charity called her and started the conversation making small talk, so my mom let her lead the call without saying much. Then Charity asked about Caleb and me. My mom cheerfully tells her we both made it home to Canada and that we had all had a magnificent Christmas celebration together. I don't know how my mom even said that. She always tells the truth and lives with the consequences. But I guess when two of her children's lives are at stake, all bets are off. This is the first time Charity has contacted us since she left Victory's. My mom tells her she cannot understand why she had acted the way she had, when we would have given her every opportunity within our means to have a life full of opportunities here in Canada. Charity tells her that Effia and Selorm had convinced her we were just lying to her the entire time, and that we had never intended to follow through with our plans to bring her to Canada. My mom then told her she would have then made a home for us somewhere in Ghana and we would have still been her greatest support just for taking care of Caleb. Out of that call the only thing that really mattered was that she believed Caleb and I had left Ghana because after that call my cell phone finally stopped ringing and I could get some sleep.

During one of our calls a few days later, my mom says that the medical report has made it to France intact! We are so excited. We'd been told that reports don't take very long to be processed; usually just a matter of days. We began to see a light at the end of the tunnel. My mom starts talking about booking flights home. It was still the Christmas holiday season around the globe, so she decided to check what sort of options we'd have, as far as flying out of Ghana in the next couple of weeks or so—she would call Mardy and let me know right away.

I was flipping through my passport while we were talking and when I saw the expiry date of my newest visa, I couldn't believe my eyes—I just stared in shock. Someone had used a black ink pen to carefully change the "6" to a "3", leaving me with a very authentic looking 30 day visa instead of the original 60 day visa I had been issued. I had less than three days to leave Ghana. The change had been done with great skill and I had no proof with me to show that I had departed from Canada with a 60 day visa. I also had no idea of who had tampered with my passport or when they might have done it. My heart is pounding so loud that I can hardly talk to my mom. I tell her about the tampering. I decide I will stay with Caleb anyway and take my chances when we boarded a flight home together. We could only guess how much longer Caleb and I would be stuck in Ghana. My mom reminded me that Effia had obvious connections at the airport. If I tried to board a plane back to Canada with an expired visa, they could detain me. It was too risky for Caleb. If they detained me, they had every right to call Effia to come for Caleb because, once again, the new document naming me as the legal representative for Caleb, still hadn't arrived. And there may still be a warrant out for my arrest for allegedly kidnapping him from Last Hope. There are too many risks for me at the airport and my mom was crying and telling me that it's a very difficult decision, but we have to take the risk that I come home first and trust that Caleb will be able to follow soon. She cannot take this anymore. She cannot even fathom what she would do if I were arrested and Caleb disappeared from the airport. She demands that I come home and calls Mardy and he sends me my ticket.

I am so very upset. Sometimes I don't think my mom understands how much Caleb and I have bonded during this time. I am all he has and every day we survive—drawing on each other. Just a smile from one to another can get us through another minute. Every day it is the two of us living in this sweltering heat with each minute taking an hour to pass. But in the end, I listen to my mom and plan to go home. I know that my mom also knows that she is asking me to leave Caleb behind and that neither of us may ever see him again. That is utterly unthinkable, but even more unthinkable for her is to think that she may never see me again on top of it. With the decision to return made, I explain to Victory and Hubert and the people at the safe house about my soon to be expired visa. They all agree with my mom, it is a terrible risk to try to leave Ghana without a proper visa. And no one knows for sure if there is still a warrant out for my arrest, so it is decided that I have to fly home as soon as possible.

As I am explaining to Caleb, yet again, that I am leaving him, I try and keep it low key for his sake. I explain that his visa would come in very soon and I show him the wrong date on mine so he could understand why I have to fly out of Ghana right away. I have left Caleb twice and returned both times. He was only six and that was enough proof for him to believe that this time was going to be just like the last two times. I'd go but I'd come back! We talked about what it was going to be like when he lived in Canada with us. Luckily, Caleb had gotten to know the people who lived at the safe house and he was comfortable with them, so he wasn't nervous about being left with them.

I cannot explain to anyone how badly my heart was breaking to have to leave him once again. That I didn't know if I'd ever see Caleb again. My cell phone had started ringing again around the clock. Obviously Effia and Selorm hadn't believed what my mom had told Charity; about Caleb and I being home already. I was terrified that they would track him down despite the vigilance of the people in the safe house. Even though they assured me over and over again, that they would take wonderful care of Caleb and not let him go outside for any reason, they could not assuage my deepest fears for him. They had no idea who these people were and what they looked like, at least I knew to watch for them, I may not know all their contacts but it was some small thing that I knew to look for them. It doesn't matter—I have to let go and go home.

I fly into Edmonton on New Year's Eve 2010 without Caleb by my side. This is the worst New Year's Eve of my life, and there was no celebrating to be done. Everyone was happy to see me home safe, and my sister was shocked that I had grey hairs from my ordeal of just over twenty days in Ghana.

My mom and I spend lots of time together. She cries a lot. She is happy I'm home safe and she says she cannot even believe how strong I was to live through that trip, but in the end it was the hardest decision of her life to tell me to leave her newly adopted son and bring her myself home to safety. I share with her that I don't think of Caleb as hers anymore. He is mine. He has always been mine right from the start. I love him enough to share him, but I want her to understand that things have changed. When Caleb comes home he will decide where he feels he needs to be. I love my mom, and our bond is very strong and very strange, but I need her to try and understand what Caleb and I have just been through.

Every day we talk for hours about everything and anything that happened in the past weeks. I say to her remember when I thought our vacation with the boys would have an adverse effect on Last Hope, as Effia had witnessed how poorly other owners provided for their wards? Well, sure enough I had seen the effects for myself. When I was living with Victory, I had to go into the village of Anagonyigba—I was trying to get an appointment with the man who oversaw local adoptions. I bumped into three of the older girls who lived at Last Hope and I was shocked. Their hair was in tangles and looked like it hadn't been washed in weeks. Their faces and hands were dirty, their clothes were filthy and needed mending and their skin was gray—which meant pomade for their skin was not being provided anymore. I think it's fair to assume that the level of care had dropped drastically at Last Hope. I believe Effia and Selorm have cut back on the care of the children to increase their profit margin.

A month ago this conversation would have perked us up and got us thinking and talking about what we could do to make changes in the systems—maybe we could get our MP to get us a formal invitation to meet with the Minister of Women and Children's Affairs (which does happen later but we don't go – it's impossible to go back to Ghana now). But there is no spark in either of us. We talk and talk but all we want is to hear that Caleb is cleared to come home to us. I love my mom and her support, but I really only want to have Caleb safe in my arms again. Where is he? What is he doing right now? Is he alone in the safe house all day now that I'm not there? Does he have to sleep alone? Is he scared? What is he thinking? Does he still believe in me? Why does no one understand what I am going through?

Canada

Starting in January 2010

Every day Caleb overwhelmed each and every thought. Each day the minutes ticked by ever so slowly and we'd wonder what he was doing and if he was safe. Several times an hour we went online to track where his medical report was and day after day, it remained at the French office. We kept in daily contact with Victory and Hubert and the people at the safe house, and spoke to Caleb each day too. He was such a good boy through this time. We couldn't be more proud of him.

Meanwhile we thought ahead to the next step of getting Caleb home on a plane unaccompanied. We talked with our travel agent, Mardy, on how we could accomplish this, and he suggested that we could fly him home on Lufthansa Airlines as an unaccompanied minor. If Effia had connections with people at the airport they would be looking for a white woman checking in with a six year old Ghanaian boy. Instead, Caleb would be taken to the airline's desk by an older Ghanaian man; one of the people who lived at the safe house. The airline staff would then take Caleb immediately to a private, secured waiting room, away from where the rest of the passengers would wait to board the plane. He would remain under the staff's close supervision until he landed in Canada. This becomes our plan of action.

Every day and my mom and I commute into work together as I still live at home, and we call Victory and Hubert as well as the safe house to talk with Caleb. It's the 6th of January and we are trying to live out our normal lives during the day. I call Victory and my mom and I can hear Baby Sam in the background. He is growing into a toddler already! God how we miss them. My mom tells Victory that we finally heard from the Canadian Consulate in Paris and they have received and processed Caleb's medical report into his file—whatever that means. We hope this indicates that his visa will be granted very soon. In light of this, she will email a form that needs to accompany all the other forms Caleb needs in order to leave the country. Also, there is an additional letter that explains why the change to his travel arrangements was necessary. My mom explains that this information needs to also get to Mr. Okeke, the man that will take Caleb to the airport when the time comes, but we don't know which email address will get it to him the fastest. She asks Victory to please find that out for us.

There will be a fee of $150.00 US to pay the airline when he checks Caleb in. My mom lets Victory know that she is sending her a money order so Mr. Okeke will have the funds when the time comes. She also states we will also need to get Mr. Okeke a copy of the travel insurance for Caleb, but that we will wait until we have a better idea of when his flight will be, before we purchase it.

The same day my mom lets me know that she has received an email from Mr. Okeke. It states that Victory contacted him. And indicated what email she should use to contact him. He promises to check it frequently. My mom says he went on to ask about the family and how we are all doing and especially how I am doing. They have all the forms ready and they are just waiting for his visa. He expresses how he is hopeful that everything will go through soon and that Caleb will be with us at last. Then, the very next day my mom receives an email that we receive with such joy mixed with an equal amount of anxiety.

Email: January 07 2010

Subject: Application for a Canadian visa

File: FXXXXXXXX

Caleb Lebbih

C/o Last Hope Children's Home

Your immigrant visa appears ready to be issued. You are asked to appear in person within 60 days at the Canadian High Commission in Accra any Monday, at 8:00 am, for visa collection. The visa will be issued the same day and will be valid for 6 months or until the expiry of your medical results, whichever is earliest. You must bring this letter with you.

Regards, Immigration Section, Accra, Ghana

We rejoice as Caleb can get his visa. But this has also gone to Last Hope.

My mom sends an email off right away to Mr. Okeke.

Email: January 07 2010

Subject: FW: Application for a Canadian visa

Hi Mr. Okeke, It looks like you will be able to take Caleb to obtain his visa first thing on Monday. He will need the attached letter from the High Commission and another set of updated passport photos. Please be very cautious when you venture out with Caleb, as the operating directors of Last Hope will automatically receive a copy of the email that his visa is ready. Hopefully they may not have a modem or Internet service anymore at Last Hope because we suspended the account. We can only keep our fingers crossed that they are not yet aware of this issue date for his visa. Hopefully Caleb will be on a plane before their paper copy arrives by mail. We are one step closer!

Lots of love, Kathy

It takes us three whole days to hear back from our contact. You cannot even imagine what was going on in our minds!

Email: January 10 2010

Subject: Caleb's visa

Hi, Kathy and family. We have got new passport pictures done for Caleb. We will be at the embassy before 7:00 a.m. on Monday morning. We will inform you the moment we have his visa in our hands and we will have the $150.00 US ready for the airline too. Love to all your family, Mr. Okeke

My mom sends a quick reply.

Email: January 10 2010

Subject: Caleb's visa

Thank you so much Mr. Okeke! We will be waiting up all night! Call us as soon as you are done. We don't care what time it is over here. We will purchase travel insurance online for Caleb when we book a flight home for him. I'll email you a copy of it, so you can print it and take it with you to the airport.

Love, Kathy

My mom is the ultimate caregiver in our family. When my great grandma was hospitalized, she went every day and read her stories. And even though all this is going on, her mom needs her to accompany her on a trip to Mexico. It is important that she goes. She made the commitment thinking that she would be back before we got word about Caleb coming home. However, on her trip down there when she is changing flights in Phoenix, I call her. They have Caleb's visa! It was officially issued on January 11 2010 at 4 pm. Mr. Okeke and Caleb arrived at 6 a.m. and waited ten hours straight, but they have it. I tell her to call Mardy, our travel agent, and get Caleb on the next flight home.

The next day I call my mom and tell her Caleb is no longer in Ghana. He's in the air. He's out of their reach. He's safe. He's finally safe! I would say that I was crying at this point, but I really don't do the emotional thing. Okay, maybe a little dust got in my eye…

On January 12 2010 my dad and I travel to Calgary, the closest immigration office to us. My dad has waited a long time to meet his new son. It seems we are waiting a long time for him to get clearance. Finally an airline employee came over to my dad and asked if he was waiting for a little boy from Ghana. We both answer with an enthusiastic, "yes!" The agent then asked if we would come and get him right away because he was trying to Kung Fu everyone just like the characters in his favorite movie, *Kung Fu Panda*. I start to laugh, here I am worried about these last steps, and he is trying to kick box and do karate chops on strangers. I know he wasn't attacking them, he was just a little boy playing a game, but I guess whoever was in charge decided it was time to give him over to us. Finally, Caleb is escorted from a secure room inside the Calgary International Airport, into my waiting arms! My dad is watching us and playing the guardian—taking care of details that I just don't care about right now. Caleb is chattering on and on. He thought the plane was a room he needed to stay in for a long time until he was allowed out again. Apparently, like any curious six year old, he thought he could wander freely throughout that huge room, so he kept getting lost on the plane and the stewardesses had to return him to his seat a few times. He said the people on the plane told him to press a button if he needed anything. Well, he said he needed ice cream. He kept pressing the button and asking for ice cream and they never brought it. When they first told him they didn't have any ice-cream, he asked if they could stop at a store on the way to Canada to get some. That cracked everyone up! He just couldn't understand that he was flying thousands of feet in the air.

It was so incredible to see Caleb again. I can't even describe the mixture of relief and happiness and love. He was just Caleb— nothing about the long plane ride had fazed him. He called my mom using my cell phone right away. Afterwards, we bundled him up in his new winter coat, and then took him outside so he could touch the snow. That was the most important thing to him. Caleb always lives in the moment! My dad was amazed when he met him. He always tells people that Caleb is so adaptive he must have come from Toronto, not all the way from Africa. He says it tongue in cheek because this little angel acts like any other six year old kid—you would never know he came from a mud hut African village because he acts like he just arrived from some other Canadian city. Once Caleb plays in the snow for a bit, which he absolutely loves, we head back to our home just outside of Stony Plain. My dad is ever the candy junky and has a bag of jujubes. He offers Caleb one and he pops it in his mouth. Then quickly spits it out and puts it back in the bag! My dad tells him you can't put something you've touched—let alone put in your mouth—back in the bag. But Caleb doesn't understand waste. If he were back at Last Hope, if he didn't want to eat something, you could barter with the other kids and get something for it, but you wouldn't waste even a tiny bite as small as this candy. He didn't know what to barter so he just put it back so someone else could eat it. He doesn't understand yet what abundance we take for granted in Canada.

On the way home we order and pick up pizza for supper. Caleb asked us if it was easy to order pizza in Canada. What he meant was, how available was pizza in Canada? He rarely saw pizza offered in Ghana. When I told him it was everywhere, and he could eat it anytime, he asked me why people would want to eat any other food if pizza was always available. He has no concept of the incredibly large diversity of delicious foods that are available to us on a daily basis when we go to a grocery store! We are going to have so much fun with him.

Caleb took in all that was new in his life with ease and confidence. He loves discovering new things. But that is in the daytime. At night, he has to sleep with me because he is terrified Selorm and Effia are going to come and steal him from us or kill him. He didn't understand that he was too far away now, for them to be a realistic threat. From the first night he came to Canada he has had really bad nightmares. He doesn't always articulate that it's Selorm and Effia, sometimes he says the sharks want to eat him. When at first I was trying to get him to bond with my dad, I would tell him to sleep in his own room and go see his papa if he woke up. But when I got up the next morning and he was sleeping on the floor by my bedroom door, my dad said I should just do whatever made Caleb feel safe. From then on out, every night he was sleeping with me. The nightmares eased off a bit, but he still needs a night light on in his bedroom because if he wakes up in the dark it freaks him out.

For the two weeks until my mom got back, you couldn't separate Caleb and me. I let him talk about anything he wanted to, but he rarely talked about the things that had happened in Ghana. He talked about sports, mostly about what was happening in the world of soccer.

When my mom returned and I told her about Caleb being afraid of Selorm and Effia, she brought our globe over to Caleb and pointed out to him where Ghana was and where we lived in Canada. Oh how he laughed and laughed and told her that he had never lived on a ball before. He simply wasn't able to comprehend the distance he had flown.

We are a close family and every day after Caleb went to sleep we would talk about what was going on. He has become very comfortable with my dad and my younger brother, Cody, that still lives at home. Still, it was very obvious to all of us, that during those last terrifying weeks in Ghana, while he and I hid in the safe house, our bond had deepened much more. Even though I wanted to move out of my parents' home to one of my own—I knew I couldn't do it until Caleb settled into our family and his school. He was going to a rural Alberta school and he was the only student there that was colored. He was a novelty and very popular with everyone and the school was very respectful. They held an international celebration and asked him to carry the flag of Ghana. They were very patient and understanding when Caleb was trying to teach the other boys you can pee anywhere because that's what he would do in Ghana. The school would tactfully share this information in order for us to make the necessary corrections and teach Caleb that Canada has different rules when it comes to sanitation and where you go to the bathroom.

When the school year ended though, I thought I should make the adjustment and move into my own apartment. At this time my mom and I were running a business together, so we were working together all day long and then going home and spending the evenings together as well. I felt I needed some space. So over the summer, because my mom would come and pick me up for work anyways, it was our decision to give Caleb a choice of who he wanted to be with, on a day by day basis. And then as fall approached, Caleb said he didn't want to go back to the 'white's' school. He didn't mean anything bad about that. He just didn't want to be the only colored student anymore. My mom and I looked into several schools in Edmonton that would have students that also came from Ghana and we finally picked one. After school started, Caleb would see me before and after school and then spend some weekends with me, but he usually went back to my parents' house to sleep overnight. By then he was sleeping in his own bed. As time went on, he started asking to stay overnight with me more and more, and eventually, he asked if he could call me Mommy. This time he wasn't using the word in the same way as he had in Ghana. He was choosing me to be his mother in every sense of the word. I was given the best gift ever. He had always called me Mandi, and my mom, Kathy. From the day he came to Canada he called my dad Papa. When I said he could call me mommy if he wanted to, he then asked what he should call Kathy. When I told him he should call her Nana he laughed and laughed and said that she would then need to start doing the cooking. We all love Caleb more than words can express, and we want him to define and strengthen his bonds within our family in whatever way works best for him. Using the names Mommy, Nana and Papa was his choice. This way works for him and we all honor that. So yes, in the eyes of our legal system he belongs to my parents. But sometimes there is something more important than the rules of a legal system. Sometimes you need to do what is right for a little boy who has been through too much already.

Caleb should be allowed to live his life in a way that makes him feel loved and nurtured. His well-being is the priority here, not what title he uses for each of us. He went through some very horrible experiences before he left Ghana. We're a family doing what we pledged to do when we had our family meetings. We agreed, irrevocably, as a family to love and support him to the best of our ability. This is Caleb's version of a family, and this arrangement is his way of being an inclusive member of our family. It's working for him now and that's all that matters.

This is all very different from the way we may have originally pictured how everything would unfold. I can't imagine loving him any more than I do, and like everyone in my family, I can't imagine my life without him. He's an incredible kid and like any kid, he needs parents, grandparents, siblings, cousins and aunts and uncles who love and support him so he can reach his full potential in life. That's what comes first, now and always!

These days Caleb is a well-adjusted child. We are proud of the hard work he's done to adapt to his life here. He would much rather be outside doing some sort of physical activity, or playing some sort of sport with someone else, instead of being indoors. The first time we put skates on him, he said he'd be playing hockey in a week, and low and behold he was! He is enrolled in various sports and we all take turns taking him to his games or practices, and of course, cheering for him and his team mates during competitions.

He loves to spend time with all members of his family, one on one, in groups and he's always very affectionate at all our family functions. On weekends, he still circulates his sleepovers with various family members and also invites friends over to join him for play-dates. We all still take turns supporting his events and taking him to cultural experiences.

He doesn't like to play with toys—I'm not sure why—if it's because he didn't have any and so doesn't know what to do with them, or if he just loves sports so much there isn't room for many other interests. He is generally happy, cuddly and loves to snuggle up with a family member to watch TV or play video games when he is indoors. He can sometimes be a little stubborn, but when we ask him to do something, he will generally do it without complaint.

We are most proud of his interest in sports, his grades in school, his rapid progress in improving his English and how happy he was to gain his Canadian Citizenship. Caleb loves his family and he loves that his name is now officially Caleb Kwame Rondeau. He loves going everywhere and doing new things. He loves trying new foods and most especially, he loves eating traditional Ghanaian foods.

People will ask him why his mom is white, and if his parents died. He willingly tells people his story. He will talk about his twin brother. And when asked, he says sometimes he misses him. When I see some volunteer posting about his brother I ask him if he wants to hear and see pictures, and he always does. But the conversation ends with him saying that his brother would not be happy here.

My mom's greatest fear that he may not bond has been eradicated. He is bonded with our entire family. He still gets anxious if he is away from me for more than a few days. He still hides food away. He stills get scared of being beaten if he thinks he has done something wrong. He still has a night light. He still has nightmares. It's part of who he is. He is a little abandoned boy from mud hut Africa that found his way into the hearts of a loving Canadian family and he has paid his dues to get there.

We have left Ghana, but Ghana hasn't finished with us yet. You don't walk in and take one of her children and then walk back out. There are prices to pay and if you didn't pay in dollars there are other ways to make you pay.

Recall that it was Charity that disclosed to my Mom that the operating directors of Last Hope had a plan to kidnap Caleb if we did not pay them GH¢40,000 cedis ($32,000 CAD). When she did that she ruined their chance at cashing in on a huge ransom, so knowing Effia and Selorm each have a dark side to them, we can only assume Charity would have been in trouble for essentially acting like a snitch. They would have blamed her for losing their chance at that much money. Victory and Hubert heard that they had insisted that Charity now owed them that much money and they had ordered her to pay it back, even if it took the rest of her lifetime.

Months passed and one day Charity received a phone call that there was a gas leak in her apartment. She had moved back to Accra at this time. Charity raced home and went inside to try and turn the gas off. Someone or something ignited the gas and the place erupted into a fire ball. Charity managed to get to the door but someone had locked her in from the outside. She was still alive when help arrived, but she died in the hospital shortly after due to her entire body sustaining extensive third degree burns.

What even prompted us to look into what happened was when Selorm sent an email out to some volunteers, and one of them forwarded it to me with a horrendous picture of Charity that was taken just hours before she died. It was extremely graphic! Here is the email (words in brackets are added to help interpret the meaning):

Dear XXX, how are you doing? We are all doing very well except a tragedy that happen to Charity three days ago. She is now attending a management school in Accra. She was living in a small apart (apartment). Just three days ago, she was on her way to school when she was called that gas was smiling, (we think she meant the word 'smelling'; Selorm's English isn't that great.) so she run back to check on her gas cylinder. It was licking (leaking) so she switches it off but not knowing the next door nabour (neighbor) has set fire in her room and was cooking as well. So when Charity opens her door to put off her cylinder, the gas started coming out. All off (of) sadden (sudden) her room cutch (catch) fire and the door got looked (locked) by itself. So she straggled (struggled) in the flame to open the door if not she will burn to ashes but thank God she was able to open the door and came out. So she was rush (rushed) to the hospital for treatment. Likely (luckily) she was able to give my phone number and I was called. Her condition now is very critical. Her insurance got burnt and all that she has. So every service at the hospital we're being paid for. (She means they are paying for her treatment.)

Now I don't have any more money left on me. The Doc asked us to deposit GH¢500 cedis after all the expenses we incurred three days ago, which was around GH¢700 cedis. We were asked to go and look for the deposit and come back yesterday, (she means come back the next day). When I got to the hospital I was told in the nite (night) her condition got worse so they have to fix the oxygen on her because she was not able to brief (breathe) well. Now we have to pay for the oxygen too. (Selorm means they had put Charity on a respirator because she could no longer breathe on her own.) I don't know what is going to be the next (going to happen) so we are appealing to u (you) all to please please for Christ sake come to the aid of Charity. Please help us save her life. The Doc told me that we may need more than GH¢1500 cedis for her treatment. Please come to our aid. Thanks for everything and God reward you.

We learned that when the police got there, Charity was inside the burning apartment. In my experience doors in Ghana don't lock themselves as it takes the key to lock them and the key to unlock them, someone had locked Charity in. They wanted her to die in that fire. Word of Charity's death travelled through the online community of volunteers very quickly from sources other than Effia and Selorm. Volunteers had already posted 'RIP Charity' on many international Internet sites days before Selorm sent out this request. She was trying to solicit money to cover hospital costs for a person who was already dead!

My mom's heart has always been a little soft where Charity is concerned and I didn't realize how much that I too bonded with her on the adoption trip. The Charity who came into our lives as a very sweet, wonderful young woman conflicts so much with the Charity who mistreated Caleb so badly and colluded with Effia and Selorm to hurt him or even murder him. My mom wanted to believe in her and to help her. And in the end, no matter what Charity did, no one deserves to die like that. If we had come up with a way to separate her from the influence of Effia and Selorm, maybe she could have turned her life around. It's just so hard and so disappointing to accept that she threw her lot in with the likes of them. Maybe she was going to management school so she could earn a better living to pay them back faster for the money she'd lost them. Who knows? It breaks my heart that she died so violently. She was so young.

To this day I wrestle with conflicting thoughts when I think back to Charity and the way she flipped from being a fantastic helper and caregiver for Caleb, to someone who had zero regard for his welfare. I keep reaching the same conclusion in my mind over and over again. I believe the operating directors asked Charity to put on an elaborate charade for the five weeks she lived with us. When my mom and I both had to leave Ghana, our options were limited and they were the ones who suggested interviewing her for the position of nanny and teacher. Charity seemed like a bright light, someone who stood out as being a wonderful person just at the right time. Based on her flawless performance of pretending to be someone she wasn't, I stand by our decision to leave her in charge of Caleb. I honestly believe no one could have picked up on her true intentions. It was an acting job worthy of an Oscar. Five weeks wasn't that long for Charity to keep up the facade of being someone so trustworthy and kind-hearted.

We didn't know she had grown up with Selorm. I think Charity had unfortunately been their puppet from day one. If we would have taken her to Canada, I think Effia and Selorm would have endlessly used her to solicit money on their behalf. I can't help wondering if once Charity got hired by us and came face to face with what must have seemed like an endless source of money that she simply got greedy and decided to skim off a pile of money for herself while she played her role in their scheme. Charity actually did end up pocketing a lot of money from us; her monthly wages and a good portion of the hefty monthly budget we'd established for her. We know that she fed Caleb cheap foods in inadequate quantities and pocketed the rest of the large amount of money that was budgeted each month to buy them both highly priced western food items. And shortly after Charity stormed out of Victory and Hubert's home, she went back to the school where Mom had prepaid $500.00 for Mary's tuition and told the school administrator that we had changed our minds and wanted our money back. (Mary was the young teen who was hired by our French friend, Henri to be his house girl). My mom received an email from Mary's brother, complaining that we had lied to their family about covering the cost of Mary's education. The school officials told him that they had given all the money back to Charity because they believed her when she told them she was there to collect it on our behalf. So in total, Charity lined her pockets with more money than she could have dreamed of making in the next ten years of her life! I think, ultimately, that she tried to play the game with the big power players, but she was simply no match for them. If she began to purchase things that were normally beyond her means to afford, Effia and Selorm would have noticed. They would have felt a huge sense of entitlement to any of our money that ended up in her pockets.

It's conceivable that Effia and Selorm had her killed to send a message loud and clear that no one helps themselves to money while they are working on behalf of the two of them. Truly, in the end we don't know why some things happened and why people made some of the decisions they made. We met good people, but now we can't help but question why they were so good to us. Were they in on this? And if so, whose side were they on? We found ourselves in a complicated game of chess with innocent children used as the pawns. Every action and decision we had to make involved playing out multiple scenarios in our mind; weighing actions and consequences. Caleb's life meant nothing to these two women. He was just a pawn in their game, no more—no less and the same can be said for Charity!

If anyone had spent the same amount of time with those two women, Effia and Selorm, like we did, you would really appreciate how dedicated they are about getting money out of people. They are masters at it. I think it's conceivable that not extorting that GH¢40,000 cedis out of us was possibly the first time they had failed to collect on one of their schemes. They ruled their business with an iron fist; the children, the volunteers, and the donations. They don't come across as people who accept failure after they set their eyes on a prize. In my opinion, and I'm only speaking for myself, I think that Charity's death was a message to all, now and in the future, that any attempts to undermine their control in any way would bring fatal consequences. Effia and Selorm lost control of the situation when Charity disclosed what she did to us, and she paid the highest price imaginable—her life! This, of course, is just my personal speculation about this incident.

After all is said and done, I did spend the summer with Charity and she was like a sister to me, and a daughter to my mom. We want nothing more than for her to rest in peace.

So, a blood price has now been paid. So why does Ghana still call to both my mom and I?

Epilogue

The Children's Home that Caleb lived in prior to being adopted is still operated by its two original directors. We remain in contact with the couple we befriended during the adoption trip and who later assisted Mandi and Caleb in the final trip. We also maintain contact with the couple that offered the safe house in Accra. We have severed all other connections in Ghana as it remains unclear who can and cannot be trusted. The grandfather made the decision to not take Caleb's siblings from the Children's Home and they continue to reside there at the time we are writing this book. We think of Etse every day. We wonder what he is doing and where he is. He hated shoes and loved bare feet. We think about the fact that he wouldn't be able to walk around in bare feet here, or play most of the day. He liked the slow, calm pace of village life where he could play all day with younger children whom he could relate to more easily. He hated school because he couldn't do it. He never minded too much if there wasn't lots of food. As long as there was a little food he was content. We fondly think of the little savage he was—eating chicken bones and spitting them out no matter where he was. He would become so sullen and pouty if we tried to correct him. He didn't want to be a little gentleman or anything else. Mandi will sometimes find pictures of Etse online or someone will give her an update on him. He's still not doing his schoolwork and he's still very small, but he's all smiles.

The young girl who was brought to the Children's Home during Mandi's first trip, who was suffering from advanced HIV and whose little brother passed away, also passed away in 2012 at the age of ten. She battled the disease with courage and dignity beyond her years and is missed dearly by all who came to know her incredible spirit and bright smile. She lives in our hearts and will always be remembered.

Donating to Third World Projects

This story was to reveal a marketing untruth. It wasn't written to shut down Last Hope or any other Children's Home projects. If that were to happen, the children could be dispersed and sent to other orphanages throughout Ghana, even though some of them have at least one parent living in or close to the village. Displaced children would be considered outsiders because they may not know the local dialect of that specific region. Each region of Ghana has one or more different dialects. In total there have been recorded as many as 250 different dialects in this small country of about 24+ million people in 92,099 sq miles (35,560 km²) – roughly the size of the UK. The worst consequence of shutting down Last Hope would be that the education of all those children would end—permanently. They would be put to work on the farms, or left in mud huts all day while their parents worked. Those who were literally orphans, would end up in slavery or child prostitution. This is why this topic is so complex. There are no easy solutions. Until the government mandates better training in childcare, better business practices and appropriate supervision of the people who want to get into this business, change will not happen. The Ghanaian government must insist on legitimate accountability for how donated funds are spent, and how donated supplies are used.

We would like to stress that education is invaluable. If the Ghanaian Department of Social Welfare were to shut down every enterprise like Last Hope, far greater numbers of children will end up illiterate. Education has always played a valuable role in the fight against poverty. All the volunteers we contacted shared their own horror stories about other Ghanaian orphanages. However, those volunteers also witnessed the poverty up close so they understand the dilemma. Last Hope is exactly that—it's the last hope for most of these children. It's not a compassionately run safe haven but it offers something—a little hope. None of the volunteers want to be responsible for taking that hope away from these children, or causing them to be displaced or have them end up in slavery or prostitution.

These children are caught up in the cogs of a very broken system that has functioned like this for a long time and is growing bigger, not smaller—it is such a lucrative business. The Ghanaian government needs to offer help to families so they can make a sustainable living that allows parents to adequately provide for their children. The government needs to provide funding for community based programs to educate women so they can enter the job market and support themselves if they become husbandless. Giving financial assistance so parentless children can stay within their extended family, and offering adequate, affordable health care and education for children will go a long ways to prevent children from ending up in places like Last Hope.

Even if it is hope built on lies or highly improbable odds, operating directors like the ones we encountered attract money, volunteers and impress the locals with their strategic staging. People in poverty are highly impressionable. It doesn't take a lot to make a big impression, like when the operating directors hijacked the food we'd bought for the big Canada Day Celebration and offered platters of free food to all the visiting students and teachers. Villagers came and watched through the chain link fence. They used our food to send the powerful message that they had more than enough food to feed all the children, plus enough left over to feed all the guests. In an area where obtaining enough food, on a weekly basis, is a constant struggle for the majority of people, it added to the perception and belief that Last Hope is a wealthy haven for children who are lucky enough to be housed there. It's as simple as that, but it's also as tragic as that.

To give this a global perspective it's been widely reported in the news on the CBC (Canadian Broadcasting Corporation) and in McLean's magazine, that orphanages, and other charity institutions in Greece, are being flooded with children because of the Greek Debt Crisis. Greek families are putting their children into state run institutionalized care because parents can't afford to take adequate care of their children. Parents are facing financial disasters of such magnitude, they believe and hope that their child may have a chance for a better life being housed in an orphanage or adopted by strangers. I think we all have to remember that poverty—long term, generational poverty—or an irreversible economic disaster, generates such intrinsic despair and hopelessness, it drives people to make unimaginable decisions that are inconceivable when all is well.

Research

A January 2009 study by the Department of Social Welfare (DSW)–responsible for children's welfare and supervision of orphanages–showed that up to 90 percent of the estimated 4,500 children in orphanages in Ghana are not orphans, and 140 of the 148 orphanages around the country are un-licensed, said the department's assistant director Helena Obeng Asamoah.

"We are alarmed at the extent to which the orphanages have abused the country's child protection laws", she told IRIN. (IRIN stands for the Integrated Regional Information Network which offers online humanitarian news and analysis through the UN Office for The Coordination of Humanitarian Affairs.)

Accra-based child protection specialist with the UN Children's Fund (UNICEF) Eric Okrah told IRIN, "Running an orphanage in Ghana has become a business enterprise, a highly lucrative and profitable venture." He added, "Children's welfare at these orphanages has become secondary to the profit motive."

In Ghana a small orphanage might have a budget of up to US $70,000 a year, depending on its size, the bulk of the funds coming from international donors and NGOs, with small contributions from local corporations, according to research by Ghanaian non-profit Child Rights International (CRI). "Donors are attracted to orphanages because they appear to be a simple solution", said Joachim Theis, UNICEF head of child protection for West Africa. "You have a building, you house children in it; it is easy to count them. And they are easy to fundraise for. It is a model that has been used for a long time. But it is the wrong model."

An article posted in May 2009 on IRIN states in part, "After researching financing in several Ghanaian orphanages, CRI's (Child Rights International) Bright Apiah surmised that as little as 30 percent of funds received are spent on child care."

African Press International on May 29, 2009 Accra (Ghana). West Africa: Protecting children from orphan-dealers–there are many unlicensed orphanage homes in Ghana.

Racism

Using the term 'whites' was in no way meant to be racist. It is used by Ghanaians to refer to foreigners, or more precisely, anyone with light colored skin who is from the Western World, or from a 1st World Country; as opposed to a 3rd World Country. When volunteers visit and work at Joe Smith's place in Ghana, they are referred to as Joe Smith's whites. When Mandi volunteered at Last Hope, if she walked into the village of Anagonyigba, and someone said hello to her, after she introduced herself they would say, "Oh yes! You are one of Effia and Selorm's whites."

There are very strict rules associated with being a white of a certain Ghanaian. As mentioned in our story, we could only deal with certain vendors when we shopped with Effia or Selorm or Jeremy. Vendors paid a percentage of what we whites spent in their shop, back to Effia and Selorm. Wherever we travelled, with or without one of them, we were still assumed to be their whites. We were also Charity's whites. Once, we went to market without her and when she went there later, people stopped her to tell her that her whites had surely been looking for her, because they were shopping on their own. She then explained to us that she needed to do the shopping otherwise it would ruin her reputation and villagers would think she was not doing her job properly. It is a label, just like the label of 'celebrity' or 'politician' except that being someone's whites carries a possessive connotation—we are their whites and the unspoken rule is that no one interferes with their control of us.

Dashing

The custom of dashing is changing in Ghana. Not everyone we encountered required dashing. The director in Ho refused to be dashed, and we only did so to keep on good terms with the operating directors. But even though the director firmly declined to be dashed, he did inform us that if his secretary did any work on our behalf, we would be expected to dash her. We have no idea how the Canadian Immigration Office (CIO) in Ghana, differentiates between dashing and bribing. It was a constant worry for us. We had to account for every penny we spent and it was very stressful to deal with the custom of dashing everyone. We always checked the price of dashing before entering a transportation vehicle because we knew the drivers would need money to cover the cost of dashing the police at checkpoints and drivers transporting whites were asked to pay more. Eventually we knew which quoted prices were reasonable.

We needed to dash a certain amount because people demanded it, but we were always afraid that Canadian Immigration would audit our expenditures, as was their right, and then accuse us of using bribery to gain an adoption. If we thought we could justify an expense (whether it was a dash or not) without a receipt, in a future audit, then we paid the amount. If we didn't think we could explain the amount, as was the case in the exorbitant fees we were quoted for our passports, we didn't pay. We simply found another way to get what we needed for our adoption application.

Donating with Ethics

We feel places like Last Hope could be an asset to local communities if they were run legitimately with trained staff. We want this book to expose people to the very high probability of donation-hijacking and the prevalence of deceptive business tactics amongst operators of most orphanages in Ghana. We want to expose how children housed in these enterprises are viewed as commodities and how their wellbeing suffers from donation-hijacking. We want people to understand that simply sending donations of money or supplies to places like Last Hope by no means guarantees that children will benefit. If donors around the world would demand accountability for how donated goods and funds are spent, business practices in this sector would improve. Ghanaian entrepreneurs, who offer transparency of how donations are used to benefit children in their care, will flourish. Those that withhold accountability will be unable to compete for business until they follow suit. Those who donate can exert tremendous pressure upon this corrupted business sector.

We want people and organizations that send donations to help children in Ghana to exercise greater discernment about who they choose to support. Everyone needs to understand that bribery is engrained in Ghanaian culture and potential donors need to face reality—70% of what they donate may be used for the personal gain of entrepreneurs running orphanages.

If you are sending supplies, send people with those supplies, to personally distribute them to your intended recipient. If you are sending mosquito nets for children's beds, have your own people actually put them up over children's beds instead of just delivering them to the orphanage in boxes. If you are sending medical supplies, send them with qualified professionals who can dispense them. Or you can donate them to legitimate clinics and hospitals instead and arrange for your representative to purchase proper medical cards for every child in the surrounding area, who does not have one. If you are donating money specifically for food, don't send the money. Send people WITH that money to buy the food locally and distribute it on a daily basis if that's what it takes to guarantee children will benefit. That way you will also be helping local farmers and vendors too. And finally, make sure you have a highly recommended translator; someone who is not connected to this business in any way. In other words, it is going to take a much greater and more focused effort on the part of donors to bypass the corruption and ensure children actually benefit but it can be done. It must be done because it's the only way to circumvent the endemic corruption.

People also need to expect to face a constant barrage of requests for more money and constant pressure from people like Effia and Selorm, who will do their utmost to gain control over the donations you might be delivering in person. Organizations need to educate themselves on the tactics of high pressure solicitations their people will undoubtedly face when they deal face to face with these types of entrepreneurs. We're not saying that these suggested strategies will stop all donation-hijacking—it won't—but it will dramatically increase the percentage of benefits that could reach the children they are intended to help.

Donors also need to do their research beforehand too! Don't rely on word of mouth unless it is from someone who did actual business with the owners of an orphanage or children's home. Don't deny that staging takes place; accept that staging is one of the strongest marketing strategies used. Don't ask volunteers if the place they visited is being run legitimately—they won't know unless they volunteered at one of these places for many, many months. Long-term volunteers that I contacted had completely different opinions of Last Hope than others who, like me, only volunteered for a couple of months

In this day and age, you haven't actually helped a child until you have taken steps to negate or prevent the hijacking of your donation. That's the new reality donors have to step into. All donors need to take it upon themselves to do their due diligence. It's the only way to truly help this situation. That's the conversation we hope our book will spark!

The Reality of Adoption

First of all, we are not condoning that adoption is the best way to help every one of these children. Adoption is not a panacea to enhance the lives of Ghana's vulnerable children and we're not advocating that it is. It was the right thing to do with respect to Caleb. It was the wrong thing to do for Etse. We believe this book will give people a realistic view of the challenges they may face if they pursue a private, legal adoption in Ghana. The culture is challenging to do business in, the requirements are challenging to fulfill, the legal work is challenging to acquire and the adoption business attracts some powerful and violent players. Our book uncovers the darkness and dangers that occur inside this business sector for anyone attempting to do what we did. And most of all, people need to realize that if someone asks for a lump sum of money to manage the legalities of a private adoption, there is a very high likelihood you are being ripped off, for lack of a better term. If you do that, as far as we are concerned, you are participating in child-trafficking.

Dead Draw

In chess, Dead Draw means the chess pieces have reached a configuration on the board that makes it impossible for either player to win. With regards to our experience, we were pitted against a system that was broken and ruled by corruption. We were forced to play a deadly game of cat and mouse to bring Caleb home safely. Did we succeed? Yes. Did we win? No. As long as there are vulnerable children in Ghana, whose lives are in the hands of greedy, uncaring entrepreneurs who use them as mere commodities to acquire money and status, no one wins.

We have all had to compromise and settle for what we could take away from this experience. Caleb has us, but he will never have his birth family again—most likely he will never be able to visit his roots in Ghana safely. We have Caleb but we know that many people have paid a high price for him to be with us—we have memories that refuse to be forgotten. Etse will grow up in his beloved Ghana, and no one can predict if he will ever make meaningful connections to people. Will he ever find people like us, people who will always love him? The directors have their children's home but they have also had to suffer direct hits to their pride and sense of status. They also have to consider making big changes to the way they do business in the future; changes that will take them far out of their comfort zone. We all have to live with the good and the bad, as well as the happiness and the sorrow that came from this experience.